Charles a

Charles and Diana

Their Married Life

by

Graham and Heather Fisher

ROBERT HALE · LONDON

© Graham and Heather Fisher 1984

First published in Great Britain 1984

ISBN 0 7090 1743 X

Robert Hale Limited
Clerkenwell House
Clerkenwell Green
London EC1R 0HT

Photoset and printed in Great Britain by
Photobooks (Bristol) Ltd.
and bound by
W.B.C. Bookbinders Ltd.

Contents

For our daughters,
Janet and Linda

Illustrations

PICTURE CREDITS

Keystone Press Agency Ltd: 1, 6, 11, 16-18, 23, 52; Popperfoto: 2, 15, 24, 27, 37-8, 48; Mr Anwar Hussein: 3, 4, 12, 19, 28, 31-6, 39-40, 42, 45, 47, 49, 51, 54, 55; Syndication International: 5, 7-10, 13-14, 20-22, 26, 29-30, 41, 43-4, 46, 50, 53; Lynn News: 25

Foreword

This book is a sequel to our earlier biography of the Prince of Wales, *Charles: The Man & The Prince*, the revised edition of which took the story up to the time of his marriage to Lady Diana Spencer. Much has happened to them since, not least the birth of their first child, Prince William of Wales.

If, in relating the story of their first few years of married life, we have fallen into the trap of focusing more on the Princess of Wales than on her husband, we crave indulgence. Not, we imagine, that many of those who read this book will fault us on that account, judging by the way people clamour to see the Princess who is so new and fresh to the royal scene.

G. & H.F.
Keston Park,
Kent

THEIR ROYAL HIGHNESSES
THE PRINCE   &   PRINCESS
OF WALES

Names:

Charles Philip Arthur George   Diana Frances (née Spencer)

Appearance:

Height: 5 feet 11 inches;
Eyes: Blue; Hair: Brown

Height: 5 feet 10 inches;
Eyes: Blue; Hair: Fair

Born:

Buckingham Palace, London,
14 November 1948

Park House, Sandringham;
1 July 1961

Parents:

Queen Elizabeth II &
Prince Philip

8th Earl Spencer & the Hon.
Mrs Frances Shand-Kydd

Educated:

Hill House, London; Cheam
Preparatory School;
Gordonstoun; Geelong Church
of England Grammar School,
Australia; Trinity College,
Cambridge; University College
of Wales

Silfield School, King's Lynn;
Riddlesworth Hall, Norfolk;
West Heath, Kent; Vie de
Manette Château d'Oex,
Switzerland

Married:
St Paul's Cathedral   29 July 1981

Son:
Prince William of Wales (William Arthur Philip Louis)
Born St Mary's Hospital, London, 21 June 1982

Residences:
Kensington Palace, London and
Highgrove, near Tetbury, Gloucestershire

1 Marriage Lines

It was the first real opportunity the newlyweds had had to entertain in their own home, to show off what they had done in the way of renovation and decoration and to display at least some of their many wedding gifts in their proper setting. There was also the thrilling news to impart that already, after only a few months of marriage, they were expecting their first child.

Happily, they took their guests on a tour of the house; showed them, among other things, the still unfurnished rooms upstairs which would serve as the baby's nursery. Then, when the time came for their visitors to leave, they walked outside to see them off, standing together, arms around each other, waving goodbye as they drove away.

It is always nice to have a visit from close friends. But it is nice too, for newlyweds, to be alone again. So, as their friends' cars disappeared from sight, they joined hands, dancing and skipping together round the lawn before going back into the house.

It could have been almost any young couple not long married and very much in love, delighting in the happiness they found in each other and rejoicing that there was a baby on the way. It happened to be the Prince and Princess of Wales.

One of the visitors that day to Highgrove, their home in the Gloucestershire countryside, was Diana's sister, Lady Sarah McCorquodale, who herself once made the headlines as a possible future Princess of Wales in the days when Charles was the world's most eligible bachelor and her youngest sister no more than a tall, leggy, netball-playing schoolgirl. Sister of the Princess, one-time girl-friend of the Prince, she knows them better than most and sees them as 'totally compatible'.

If 'totally' is perhaps to overstate their compatibility somewhat, it is surely not by all that much. That they are very much in love there can be no doubt. It is to be seen in the tenderly affectionate glances they so constantly exchange; in the way they hold hands and even kiss in public; in the way Diana cuddles up to her husband and leans her head on his shoulder, and in the affectionate pat he is sometimes seen to administer to her bottom. Charles was at the bedside, a comforting and supportive husband, when Diana gave birth to their first child, a fact which strengthened and deepened the pair-bond between them. Both dote on 'Wills', their affectionate pet-name for their small son, and, on their own admission, are sometimes apt to spoil him. In the words of Diana's father, Earl Spencer, 'They are crazy about him.' Diana, on royal walkabouts, has shown herself eager to tell people how 'Wills' is coming along. So, for that matter, has Charles, even if, man-like, his comments are sometimes more jokey than hers. And his public speeches, these days, seem curiously incomplete if they do not include at least a passing reference to his wife, his son or both. 'My dear wife', he has termed Diana on more than one occasion. And if he has not actually spoken of the love he feels for her, it shows through.

In many ways the two of them are curiously alike, not least emotionally. Both laugh and cry easily. Certain passages of music, Charles has confessed, can move him to tears, while it is a matter of public record that Diana broke down and wept over the death of his horse Allibar. At the other end of the scale, it was perhaps fortunate that both were facing the same way and thus did not meet each other's eyes when a splendid flourish on the part of the choirmaster sent a lampshade flying or the solemnity of their wedding ceremony in St Paul's Cathedral might have been marred by an unscheduled fit of giggling. Along with a shared sense of humour goes a ready wit. 'Perhaps I can bring a reporter down with it,' Charles quipped when presented with a boomerang during their tour of Australia. 'Is it for Prince Charles or our baby?' Diana queried, impishly, when given a prince-sized teddy bear on a visit to Canterbury.

Both are tolerant and forbearing. If Diana was the type to lose her temper, there was surely reason enough in all the newspaper harassment she suffered in the months leading up to marriage. She never did. Hurt and distressed rather than angry, she remained patient and polite always. But the memory lingers, perpetuated and accentuated by some of the things which have since appeared in print. Her father-in-law, Prince Philip, has conditioned himself to read what the newspapers say about him as though it refers merely to 'some animal in a zoo'. Or so he maintains. Diana has not yet reached that stage of royal conditioning—nor is she ever likely to—and still 'suffers agonies' at some of the things written about her. And the privacy of married life is sometimes marred for her by a fear of lurking photographers. If Diana has never been known to lose her temper, Charles has. Stupid remarks about his parents made during the commentary on a polo game in Nassau once saw him barge, red-faced and angry, into the commentary box. But he was a much younger man at the time and there has been nothing similar in the more than ten years since. Occasionally he will snap an answer to some reporter or photographer, but that is as far as it goes.

Neither husband nor wife smokes, and both are abstemious. They have many shared interests: their small son, music, painting, skiing, swimming. It was their shared love of music which caused them to pick St Paul's rather than Westminster Abbey for their wedding. St Paul's, they thought, had the better acoustics. They share too a love of country life. If he had not been born to be King, Charles has said, he would like to have been a farmer. 'I am a countryman. I can't stand cities.' Diana was born and brought up in the country, amidst the woods and flat fields of Norfolk. 'I hated to be indoors,' she says, recalling her childhood. Indeed, she was something of a tomboy in those days, according to childhood friends. But tomboyishness in childhood has not developed into an enthusiasm for such aspects of country life as huntin', shootin' and fishin'. True, her husband taught her the art of casting a fly during their courtship days and, prior to pregnancy, she was persuaded to take up riding again, the first time she had been on a horse since she was thrown and broke an arm at the age of nine. But such things do not enthuse her as they do Prince Charles. Nor perhaps is she completely happy at his new-found enthusiasm for riding to hounds. As a rider, he has something of a record of spills and falls, and, wife-like, she worries.

Married life, to date, has been largely divided between Highgrove, their Georgian country house in Gloucestershire, and a large apartment at Kensington Palace, where Diana's other sister, Jane, whose husband, Robert Fellowes, is assistant private secretary to the Queen, also has an apartment. If Kensington Palace is perhaps more of a working base, Highgrove is very much a private home, though of necessity work intrudes from time to time even here. Their private life is not lived by the calendar to quite the same extent as with previous royal generations. While they still observe the more or less traditional royal round, Christmas at Windsor with others of the family, Sandringham for the New Year, Balmoral in summer, there is also the occasional break from tradition as well as from routine, Europe for winter skiing, the Caribbean for a sun-tan.

Seen together on public occasions, they make a strikingly well-matched pair. Height helps, of course. Prince Charles stands 5 feet 11 inches and the Princess is only an inch less. Indeed, with her hair piled up and topped by a tiara, she can sometimes give the impression of being the taller of the two. And she is not only tall but slim with it, with elegantly long legs inherited from her mother's side of her family tree. Her principal assets, according to Stephen Barry, her husband's ex-valet are her height, her eyes (which are blue), her smile and her complexion. More important even than these is her personality, an irresistible combination of charm, vulnerability and joy of living. 'A girl of special qualities', one of her godmothers has termed her. Few would disagree with that, though it is perhaps less easy to analyse and define these qualities. Her father, Earl Spencer, sees her as someone who is 'a giver rather than a taker'. A former school-teacher remembers her as, if not the brightest in class, always 'the girl who tried hardest'. Old friends recall other qualities: 'warm and sympathetic' . . . 'impulsive and demonstrative' . . . 'something of a romantic' (as Prince Charles has confessed he is also) . . . 'independent without being a women's libber'.

All can be accused of bias, of course. But facts bear out opinions. 'Impulsive and demonstrative' even as a small girl, she threw her arms round the neck of the judge who awarded her pet guinea-pig a prize in the local fur and feather show and kissed him. A 'giver rather than a taker' even in schooldays when she volunteered to pay weekly visits to lonely old folk in the area and to a local centre for the handicapped. Independence showed in her decision, with which Charles concurred, not to promise to obey him on her wedding day. And the way she has stood up since to the ordeal of the royal round, more stressful for her at times than anyone except Prince Charles has realized, marks her still as the girl who tries hardest.

If Prince Charles, in public, follows his father's advice to 'stand up straight and look people straight in the face', Diana does not always do the same but will tilt her head slightly and peep out at the world through lowered eyelashes. Family photographs reveal it as a trait dating from early childhood. Now, as then, it gives her an air of vulnerability, an image of porcelain delicacy. On her wedding-day, in a dress of antique lace and ivory silk taffeta with balloon sleeves and crinoline skirt, she looked every inch a Royal Doulton figurine come to life.

The wedding of Charles Philip Arthur George, Prince of Wales, and Lady Diana Frances Spencer was a combination of state ceremonial, tribal rite and musical extravaganza complete with state trumpeters, three orchestras, two choirs and guest soprano. It was also a television spectacular seen by an estimated three-quarters of a billion people in fifty-five countries. It all happened on 29 July 1981, four weeks exactly after the bride had celebrated her twentieth birthday. The venue was St Paul's, the first time a Prince of Wales had ever been married in the present cathedral. The last such wedding, more than four centuries earlier, had been in the old St Paul's, later destroyed in the Great Fire of London.

The bridegroom, resplendent in naval uniform, was married from Buckingham Palace, which is both his parents' home and the seat of Britain's monarchy; the bride from the Queen Mother's home at Clarence House nearby, a fact which afforded the convenience of the same processional route. Thousands camped out along it overnight to ensure themselves a front-row view, and by the time the bride left Clarence House, looking more figurine-like than ever in the famous royal Glass Coach, it was estimated that a million people thronged the route.

The bridegroom's two younger brothers, Prince Andrew and Prince Edward, served as his 'supporters', a term peculiar to royal marriages. Princess Margaret's daughter, Lady Sarah Armstrong-Jones, was chief bridesmaid, manipulating the bride's lengthy train with rehearsed deftness. Four other bridesmaids and two pageboys in miniature naval uniform of bygone days completed the bridal entourage. There were 2,600 guests in the cathedral, more of them from the bridegroom's side than from the bride's. Being so limited in the matter of wedding invitations had made it 'rather difficult on my side', she revealed. Still, it made for an impressive gathering of monarchs and ex-monarchs, princes and princesses from all parts of Europe as well as the Middle and Far East, not forgetting the massive King of Tonga who wisely had his own king-sized chair shipped to Britain and installed in the cathedral for the occasion.

The ring which Charles slipped on his bride's finger was fashioned from the same lump of Welsh gold that had earlier provided his mother's wedding ring. Unlike his sister, Princess Anne, who married in the name of Mountbatten-Windsor, Charles elected to use no surname on his wedding day. He was entered in the St Paul's marriage register as His Royal Highness The Prince of Wales and signed it 'Charles P'.

The marriage ceremony and the wedding 'breakfast' over, the day reached its emotional climax with that televised shot of the newlyweds kissing on the palace balcony. The total cost of the day's proceedings was said to be in the region of £½ million, but at least the bride's father did not have to foot the bill. 'Thank God for that,' said Earl Spencer.

Whatever her husband's surname, there was no mystery about the title Diana assumed on marriage: Princess of Wales. She would not be 'Princess Diana', Buckingham Palace emphasized, though conceding that most people would probably call her that just the same (as indeed they do). But constitutionally she is Princess of Wales rather than Princess Diana because, unlike Princess Anne and Princess Margaret, she is a member of the Royal Family by marriage and not by birth.

She and Charles are perhaps only the second Prince and Princess of Wales in Britain's long history who can honestly be said to have married for love. Which is not to say that the Queen and the Queen Mother did not also marry for love. But neither of them was ever Princess of Wales. When the Queen was an eighteen-year-old princess, Pwllheli town council petitioned her father, King George VI, to proclaim her Princess of Wales. He declined to do so. A stickler for royal protocol, he insisted (correctly) that that was a title reserved for the wife of the Prince of Wales. Having no son on whom he could bestow the title, there could be no Prince of Wales at the time and therefore no Princess of Wales. And King George VI himself was never Prince of Wales. That title belonged to his elder brother who later reigned briefly as King Edward VIII before abdicating to become the Duke of Windsor. So the Queen Mother, when she married the Queen's father in the 1920s, became Duchess of York, not Princess of Wales.

Before that, Princes of Wales invariably took brides selected less for love than for a variety of other reasons, for their dowries or their child-bearing potential, for their suitability to serve as future queen consorts or to cement some royal alliance. To find another Prince and Princess of Wales who married for love it is necessary to go all the way back to the fourteenth century and the Black Prince. He married his cousin, Joan.

The Black Prince was the second Prince of Wales. But Joan was the first Princess of Wales, because her royal father-in-law was apparently never created Prince of Wales while his father, the first Prince of Wales, did not marry until after being crowned King Edward II. Similar twists of historic fate, with some Princes of Wales dying unmarried while others did not marry until after they had succeeded to the crown, have resulted in Prince Charles being the twenty-first Prince of Wales while the earl's daughter who is now his wife is only the ninth Princess of Wales.

The love story of the latest Prince and Princess of Wales has about it the flavour of one of those romantic novels for which Diana's step-grandmother, Barbara Cartland, is so well known. Love first burgeoned a full year before Diana was to figure in the headlines as a possible bride for the Prince of Wales. It was the summer of 1979. As always, the Royal Family spent the holiday in Scotland, at Balmoral. Among those accompanying the Queen was her assistant private secretary, Robert Fellowes, and his wife, Diana's sister. So Diana too was invited along as youthful company for Prince Andrew.

On 27 August the Royal Family was stunned, shocked, by news of the brutal murder of Earl Mountbatten. Charles, especially, was grief-stricken at the death of a man who had been almost like a grandfather to him, and Diana, touched by his grief, sought to comfort him. She was just turned eighteen at the time, no longer the leggy schoolgirl Charles had briefly encountered in a ploughed field during a visit to her ancestral home two years before, and, in the aftermath of grief, he found himself looking at her with fresh eyes.

Little by little, over the course of the next year, their

relationship grew steadily closer, and the following summer found them once more together at Balmoral, Charles again with his parents and Diana again accompanying her sister. That they were vouchsafed the solitude necessary to gauge the true depth of their feelings for each other was thanks to a romantic conspiracy hatched by the Queen Mother, for long a close friend of Diana's maternal grandmother, Ruth, Lady Fermoy. When the others of the Royal Family dispersed at the end of the long summer stay, she invited Diana to be her guest at Birkhall, her holiday home on the Balmoral estate. At the same time Charles himself slipped back secretly to Balmoral, that romantic setting where his parents had pledged themselves to each other a generation before.

'It was planned like a military operation,' Charles recalls. But even Balmoral's romantic atmosphere proved insufficient to bring Charles to the point of proposing. Fearing possible rejection, he sought refuge in procrastination, and their Scottish idyll ended with love implied but marriage unstated.

Back in London, Charles continued his wooing, giving a false name which deceived no one if he called Diana on the telephone and one of her flatmates answered, arranging further secret meetings in an increasingly forlorn attempt to avoid the inevitable headlines. At one stage of their courtship Charles sought to ascertain Diana's views on marriage in roundabout fashion as they walked together in a friend's garden. 'If someone were to ask you . . . what would you think?' The obvious transparency of the question is said to have tickled her sense of humour, resulting in an answering giggle. It was not until shortly after Christmas that Charles finally braced himself to pop the question. Even then, he has said, he did not anticipate an immediate answer. He knew she was going on holiday to Australia with her mother and stepfather and wanted to give her a chance to 'think things over'.

Diana, however, had no need to think things over. Like the Queen, for whom it had been love the moment she first saw the young naval cadet to whom she has been happily married now for so many years, Diana had been at least a little in love with Charles ever since his visit to Althorp three years before, and she accepted him without delay or equivocation.

For Prince Charles, marriage came at the right time. A few more years might have seen him turning into something of a staid, if not crusty, bachelor. With his thirty-third birthday visible on the horizon, he was almost the same age as his warrior predecessor, the Black Prince, when he married. Diana, however, was only just turned twenty, nearly thirteen years younger than Charles, and the same degree younger than the widowed Joan was when she became the first-ever Princess of Wales. She has brought to her new role, and into the life of Prince Charles, the freshness and vitality of youth. And some of her spontaneity was quickly to rub off on her husband. But if Charles has gained from marriage, so too has she. He represents a stabilizing influence and a sense of total emotional security which she had perhaps not known since her parents' own marriage disintegrated when she was a child of six. In the years since, she has remained close to both parents, sharing herself between them, but she can hardly have known that same sense of family strength and unity which Charles derived from the rock-solid marriage of the Queen and Prince Philip.

Entry into the Royal Family has wrought no outward change in the one-time kindergarten teacher. She has become neither pushing nor arrogant, as some young ladies elevated to so illustrious a position might have done. Her father says that he sees one small change in her. She is 'not shy any more'. Not everyone would agree. She still blushes easily. But clearly she is less shy, far less uncertain, than she was. It could be that, given time, she will change the Royal Family more than it changes her. Her father would seem to think so.

'She is a very determined young woman,' he has been quoted as saying. 'I know the Royals can appear to swallow people up when others marry in and the other family always looks as if it had been pushed out, but that could never happen with us. We can cope with the pressures. We have been brought up with royalty and there is no question of us being pushed out. Diana would not permit it to happen, and she always gets her way.'

If anyone has been 'pushed out' so far, it would seem to have been Prince Charles, at least on public occasions. Private life, of course, may be somewhat different. But in public, when the two of them are together, it is Charles who has found himself taking something of a back seat. Wherever they go, whether in Britain or Australia, New Zealand or Canada, it is 'Di', as people affectionately call her in defiance of the Buckingham Palace edict, whom everyone clamours to see. Her husband takes it in

good part, is proud of it even, jokes about it, claiming that he
wishes he had two wives like her, one to take each side of the
royal walkabout while he merely directs operations. He has
commented too on the effect she produces in otherwise quite
normal people. Her every appearance is greeted with frenzied,
almost hysterical enthusiasm more suited to a goddess than a
flesh-and-blood princess, more adulation than admiration.

In Wales she was almost tugged off her feet, so eager were
people to touch her, grasp her hand. In Canada, her appearance
resulted in such a highly charged emotional atmosphere that
teen-aged girls and middle-aged mums alike were reduced to
tears. In Australia, crowds of up to 200,000 people fought to get
near her. There had been nothing like it since the Beatlemania
of the 1960s. But the root cause of the Dianamania of the 1980s,
according to psychiatrists, is totally different, a desire for
stability rather than an urge for rebellion. Professor Gerald
Sarwer-Foner, who occupies the Chair in Psychiatry at Ottawa
University, explained it this way at the time of the royal tour of
Canada: 'The fervour is similar to that which engulfed the
Beatles, but the reasons behind it are entirely different. This
hero-worship of the Royal Family shows a greater need for
reverence in today's society. People see the Prince and Princess
as figures of stability and, through the birth of Prince William,
reinforcing the concept of family life.'

That Diana is indeed a girl of 'special qualities', as her
godmother says, is shown in the way she has faced up to and
responded to the frenzied adulation which greets her wherever
she goes. No previous member of the Royal Family, not even the
Queen, has ever been called upon to face a public spotlight so
glaring and at such close quarters. Yet the nervous and
uncertain girl who, the weekend before her wedding, fled a polo
ground in tears, has proved herself well able, since marriage, to
take crowds, cameras and all the rest of the ballyhoo of the royal
roadshow almost in her stride. On her own admission, it has not
always been easy for her. There were times, early on, when she
found it 'difficult' and one occasion, in Australia, when her
nerve failed her. But for the most part she has coped excellently
and even gives the impression of actually enjoying the whole
frenetic business of royal tours, something which is not always
easy even for those brought up from childhood in the royal
tradition. As a married princess, the Queen had still to be

reminded by her mother of the necessity to smile in public, and even after succeeding to the throne the emotional tension she experienced on public occasions continued to show from time to time in hands so tightly clenched that it seemed her gloves would split at the seams.

Her daughter-in-law does not wear gloves as protection against the scrapes and scratches which can result from shaking a multitude of hands. Nor, so far, has she copied the special, and rather limp, handshake which the Queen employs to lessen the risk of crushed fingers. Diana's grasp is 'a real handshake—not like a dead fish', one New Zealand woman said after meeting her. More than most, that woman was in a position to judge. She was blind and could gauge the personality of the Princess only from the clasp of her hand. Royal hand-shaking used to be restricted to formal occasions. Where Charles and Diana are concerned, it has become decidedly informal. And there is much more of it. Swollen hands are not unknown at the end of a long, hard day on tour. However, the more experienced Charles has a remedy for that: a long soak in cold water.

If good strong hands are essential on today's royal walk-abouts, so is the ability to make small talk. The Queen has never been very good at small talk and, in her younger days, would sometimes dry up completely. Then it was the more talkative Prince Philip to the rescue. There is no occasion for Prince Charles to dash to the rescue of his Princess in similar fashion. With her arrival on the public scene, royal walkabouts have also become royal talkabouts. No previous princess has ever talked so freely and so fully—about herself, what she eats, what she wears, about her husband, about their small son. Much of what she says may seem joking and inconsequential, but it becomes a treasured memory to those to whom it is said. She is especially good with small children, the very old and the disabled, quick to take a baby in her arms or crouch down to bring herself on a level with someone confined to a wheelchair. What she says is intended for the person or persons to whom she addresses herself, and she does not like reporters dogging her footsteps so closely as to eavesdrop on her conversation. Few will fault her for that, even if, in Canada, she did threaten to kick a boom microphone which was stuck out between the legs of the crowd in her direction. If she does have a fault, it is the very feminine one of not always being as punctual on public

occasions as she might be. She is in good company. The Queen
Mother has been known at times to exhibit the same small
failing.

The new degree of informality which Charles and Diana have
brought to the royal scene is not entirely of her making (though
she has done much to emphasize and extend it). Nor, in at least
one respect, is she quite as informal as her husband. The kissing
which these days seems to be an almost obligatory part of the
Prince's itinerary began when he was little more than a
schoolboy. He was seventeen and had touched down in Hawaii
on his way to further schooling in Australia when an uninhibited
American girl, entrusted with the task of garlanding him with
the traditional *lei*, seized the opportunity to give him his first
public kiss. 'My, he is growing up,' said his mother when she
heard. The idea caught on, and throughout his bachelor life
Charles was kissed around the world. And he himself sometimes
did the kissing. As a married man, he continues to be kissed,
even if girls these days tend to ask permission first and he,
husband-like, looks to his wife for her approval. She can hardly
withhold it. She, on the other hand, prefers to pick and choose
for herself those on whom she bestows kisses. In New Zealand,
however, where she was initiated into the ancient Maori custom
of 'nose-kissing', the choice was not hers. Nevertheless she
entered into the spirit of such occasions with enthusiasm and
Charles, later, publicly praised her for having proved herself as
good as any woman when it came to 'hong-ing'. But she does not
approve of stolen kisses. 'You are supposed to shake hands,' she
blushingly reprimanded a twenty-year-old youth who took
advantage of one walkabout to plant a kiss on her cheek.

To a large extent, the couple's personal life to date
has been dominated by their small son, William, watching
him grow, observing the transformation from baby to small boy.
Because the joys of parenthood are fleeting and transient, it is
hardly to be wondered at that they should wish to be with him as
much as possible. This natural desire to be together as a family
unit has resulted in something of a break with recent royal
tradition. Father and small son, though they are respectively
first and second in line of such succession to the throne,
frequently fly together in the same aircraft, something which
did not happen when the Queen was heir to the throne and
Charles, as a child, next in line. Neither did the Queen and

Prince Philip take their small son on tour with them as Charles and Diana have already taken William; nor did they have him with them in Malta when Philip was based there as a naval officer.

The impression given in some quarters was that it was Diana who insisted on taking the baby to Australia and New Zealand with them; that she had to plead her cause and fight her corner. The facts are somewhat less dramatic. There was no palace conflict, no maternal obduracy on Diana's part or opposition from royal officials. Almost from the moment that planning for the tour (earlier postponed because of Diana's pregnancy) was set in motion again, it was tacitly assumed that William would be accompanying his parents. Prince Charles wanted their baby with them just as much as his wife did. As a child himself, he was, for a variety of reasons, often separated from his parents and sometimes for quite lengthy periods. In those days it was thought more unsettling for a child to be uprooted from familiar surroundings than to be parted from its parents. So Charles stayed behind when his mother joined his father in Malta, when his parents went to Canada on a royal tour which the Queen's father was too ill to undertake, again when they set off on the intended Australia and New Zealand tour which was abruptly cut short by the King's death, and yet again during the long six months they were touring the Commonwealth in the aftermath of the Queen's coronation. He was left in good hands, of course. There was a nanny who doted on him, Granny (the Queen Mother) to keep an eye on things and, before he was two, a small sister for company. All the same, he missed his parents—as they missed him and Anne.

The decision to take William with them to Australia and New Zealand posed problems, of course, not least how this could best be achieved without unsettling his essential daily routine. Clearly he could not be toted from place to place like an item of royal baggage as the tour ran its course. The problem was resolved by the idea of setting up a 'nursery base' in each country, Australia and New Zealand, where William could stay with his nanny and where his parents could join him in the intervals between public engagements.

If Diana's very natural attachment to her firstborn was only partly responsible for the decision to take William with them, nevertheless it represented a fundamental change in royal thinking. Doubtless there will be others. Just as the Queen was influenced by Prince Philip in the matter of royal education—it was his idea that their children should go to school—so Prince Charles cannot help but be influenced by his wife's ideas and attitudes, as her father sees clearly. Prince William, he has said, 'will grow up close to the Spencer side of the family and influenced by them as much as by the Royals'.

Diana, of course, will not be the first person who has married into the Royal Family and caused it to change. Prince Philip's influence has changed it greatly. On a personal level, over the more than sixty years since she married into it, the Queen Mother has changed it even more, turning it from the often divided family it was into the close-knit and united family it is today. There is much about the young Princess of Wales which is curiously reminiscent of the Queen Mother as she was at the same age, the same warm and giving personality and, behind the warmth, a sense of firm resolution. Not many people perhaps are old enough, and certainly not close enough to the Royal Family, to draw the comparison. One who is puts it this way: 'It is quite amazing how they both seem to project the same aura.'

The Queen Mother too was the youngest daughter of an earl when she married the Queen's father, then Duke of York, in the 1920s. Like Diana, she immediately brought a fresh and youthful vitality to the public life of the Royal Family. Nor has that youthful zest faded with the years; it has been sustained long after the time when the whole business of public appearances ceased to be new and novel to her. To Diana, of course, the royal round is still very new; novel enough for her to pop her placecard into her handbag at a public function and take it home with her.

Of the Queen Mother it has been said that she 'made a King of a husband who never expected to become one'. Diana has no such task ahead of her. Prince Charles has been aware of his kingly future and, in a sense, trained towards it since he was a small boy. But already Diana's influence has made itself felt on the relationship between Monarchy and Commonwealth. Australia's recently elected Labour Government was thinking in terms of turning the country into a republic when she and Charles went there in the spring of 1983. Indeed, had their tour not been already scheduled when the new Government took office, it might never have taken place. But take place it did, and such was the effect on the Australian people of the Royal Family's latest recruit that the Government's republican aspirations became a lost cause, at least for the immediate future. Whatever the Government might want, however the Australian Parliament might vote, it became increasingly clear as the tour progressed that the vast majority of the Australian people would give a resounding 'No' to republicanism when it came to the mandatory referendum. 'It's enough to make a republican weep,' said a man in Melbourne, where a staggering 200,000 people jammed the city centre in their desire to see Diana and Charles. And Sir William McMahon, the country's former Liberal prime minister, summed things up this way: 'Prospects of success for republicanism are remote. If it went to a vote, then looking as far ahead as you could possibly predict, the people of Australia just wouldn't have it.'

Like the Queen Mother—Queen Elizabeth as was—Queen Diana-to-be comes of sturdy stock. The first Spencer of real note made his fortune raising mutton in the days of Henry VIII. The subsequent rise of the Spencers was on a scale to merit one of those family sagas which make such addictive televiewing. That the youngest of the 8th Earl's three daughters should have married a future King is not quite the fairy story it seems. Nor is it necessarily surprising that she should have adapted so quickly and competently to her new role as Princess of Wales. If Charles was a handsome and adventurous Prince Charming when he first came into her life, she was hardly in the true Cinderella tradition. If he can trace his ancestry back to the warrior kings of Saxon England, she can at least claim to have brought the blood of the Stuarts back into the royal line. Two of her ancestresses were the mistresses of that merry, and lusty, monarch, Charles II while a third was similarly the mistress of his brother, James II.

Such vagaries of history apart, it is hardly to be wondered at that she should display 'the knowledge and sense' of the royal scene which Prince Charles, in more youthful days, once said he was seeking in his future wife. Diana's father was not exaggerating when he said, 'We have been brought up with royalty.' Few other families in Britain so abound with royal connections. From the 8th Earl himself, who was equerry to the Queen and her father before her in the days when he was a young viscount, all the way back to a distant ancestor who loaned money to Charles I to finance the royalist cause in the

Civil War, Spencers are to be found as aides, advisers, friends of successive monarchs. Diana herself was born in a house on the royal estate at Sandringham. The Royal Family, even if they lived a few fields away and were not at Sandringham all that often, were her parents' nearest neighbours. Her two sisters and a brother born later all had members of the Royal Family as godparents, though, rather ironically, she herself did not. Her upbringing was only fractionally less grand than that of her husband. She had a nanny in childhood, as her own baby does today, and later a governess. Like her present home, Highgrove, her childhood home at Sandringham had its complement of servants, butler, housekeeper, maids, chauffeur, gardeners. Going there was 'rather like going to stay with royalty', one childhood friend recalls.

Charles, nearly thirteen years her senior, was already away at boarding school when Diana was born on 1 July, 1961. In childhood those thirteen years formed a gulf too vast to bridge. But his brothers, Andrew and Edward, were more of an age with her, and she met and played with them at children's parties, though the story that they climbed a wall to ask if they could have a swim in her family's pool is no more than a myth. The pattern of her education closely resembled that of Prince Charles, a private day school followed by boarding schools. He went on to university; she to a finishing-school in Switzerland. And if Charles returned home on holiday to Buckingham Palace, she spent her holidays—once her father had succeeded to the earldom—at Althorp, her family's ancestral home, as grand today as it was in the seventeenth century when John Evelyn described it in his diary as 'such as may become a grand prince'.

So she is hardly a Cinderella. Nevertheless, love and destiny have transmuted her from the youngest daughter of an earl, a girl who worked part-time as a kindergarten teacher, into Her Royal Highness the Princess of Wales, third lady in the land after the Queen and Queen Mother, herself the future Queen and mother of the future King William V. And that is perhaps something of a fairy story in its own right.

2 Honeymoon

The newlyweds passed their first night together at Broadlands, the Mountbatten home in Hampshire. A Sunday newspaper story prior to marriage of a night, or part of one, spent together aboard the royal train, had been promptly and angrily denied—in triplicate—by Charles, by Diana—'The story was completely false'—and not least by the Queen, who was quick to defend the good name of her future daughter-in-law by saying that she took 'grave exception' to the report.

It was at Broadlands, a generation before, that the Queen and Prince Philip also spent the first night of their honeymoon, perhaps in the selfsame room with its four-poster bed and its windows looking out to the salmon waters of the River Test. To ensure honeymoon privacy for the newlyweds of 1981, police with dogs patrolled the perimeter of the 6,000-acre estate. However, a bunch of skylarking youngsters managed to breach security by scaling the high wall which surrounds the estate, but they were quickly intercepted and escorted away. So was a photographer who tried to get within camera range of the Broadlands windows by wriggling his way through dense undergrowth.

It is one of the penalties of being born royal or marrying into the Royal Family that personal privacy almost ceases to exist. Reporters and photographers are constantly trying for a scoop, pictorial or otherwise. The security men whose task it is, amongst others, to keep them at bay are themselves frequently within earshot. Also within seeing and hearing distance for much of the time are ladies-in-waiting, equerries and secretaries, valets, maids and footmen. Total privacy is a rare and precious commodity. But at least Charles and Diana, on their first night, did not have to undergo the sort of embarrassing ordeal heaped upon some royal newlyweds of the past. It is on record that when an earlier Prince of Wales, Frederick, son of George II, and his

bride Augusta retired for their first night, the rest of the Royal
Family went with them to their bedroom. The King helped his
son into his nightshift while the Queen and her daughters
prepared the bride for bed. When both were safely tucked in,
'everybody passed through the bed-chamber to see them.'

Charles and Diana had travelled to Broadlands by train from
Waterloo, the bride having changed from her wedding-dress
into a coral pink outfit of slim side-slit skirt and bolero jacket
with a matching tricorne hat festooned with ostrich feathers.
The Lord Chamberlain, Lord Maclean, who was waiting at
Waterloo to see them off, doubtless expected thank-you
handshakes from the couple for his part in masterminding the
wedding-day arrangements. To his surprise, the bride rewarded
him with more than a mere handshake. As spontaneously as she
had once kissed the Sandringham judge who awarded her pet
guinea-pig first prize in a local fur and feather show, Diana
leaned forward and kissed Lord Maclean. It was 'a lovely
surprise', he recalls. There was a kiss too for his Comptroller,
Lieutenant-Colonel Johnston.

The newlyweds emerged briefly from the privacy of
Broadlands the following morning for a stroll in the grounds,
holding hands as they walked and looking 'very happy', as
indeed they had every reason to be. In love, but not a couple to
live totally in each other's pockets, as was seen later in the day
when Charles, using the rod which had belonged to his
murdered 'grandfather', Earl Mountbatten, wandered down to
the river on his own for a spot of fishing.

They remained only three nights at Broadlands. To have
stayed longer would have involved a Sunday and the obligation
to attend morning service in Romsey Abbey, as the Queen and
Prince Philip did on their honeymoon. The result in 1947 was a
near riot, with the service constantly interrupted as more and
more people forced their way into the abbey while those unable
to do so scaled ladders, stood on chairs and even, of all things,
climbed on a sideboard to peer through the windows. Doubtless
told of all this by the bridegroom's parents, Charles and Diana
opted to leave Broadlands on the Saturday, driving to Eastleigh
Airport where an elderly twin-engined Andover of the Queen's
Flight was waiting to fly them to Gibraltar. Charles himself did
most of the piloting.

The idea of boarding the royal yacht *Britannia* at Gibraltar for

a honeymoon cruise of the Mediterranean was the cause of the
only real hiccup in the wedding arrangements. That problems
would arise should have been foreseen, if not by Charles himself,
at least by those whose job it is to advise on such things. The
Spanish dictator, General Franco, had objected years before
when Charles, at that time newly graduated from Dartmouth as
an acting sub-lieutenant in the Royal Navy, had flown to
Gibraltar to join his first ship, the guided-missile destroyer
Norfolk. The row over Spain's claim to 'The Rock' has continued
to simmer since, and Franco's successor, King Juan Carlos,
whatever his personal feelings as a distant relative of Britain's
Royal Family, had felt obliged to change his mind about
attending the wedding once it became known that Gibraltar
was to form a part, however small, of the honeymoon itinerary.
Gibraltar has been officially British since the Treaty of Utrecht in
1713, but Spain lays claim to it and has long wanted it back.
Unfortunately for Spanish hopes, the inhabitants of Gibraltar,
when it came to a referendum, voted by 12,138 to 44 to remain
British. Two years later Spain instituted an economic blockade
of the place which was still in force at the time the wedding
invitations were sent out. So news that the royal couple would
start their honeymoon cruise from Gibraltar brought an
immediate official protest from the Spanish Government. The
use of a Spanish port was offered as an alternative. 'No, thank
you,' said Britain. With all this political furore going on, King
Juan Carlos, having previously accepted an invitation to the
wedding—his name was already printed in the official
programme—felt that Spanish pride now required him to stay
away.

However, Spanish threats of blockading Gibraltar with boats
and staging a mass protest at the frontier which separates
Gibraltar from the Spanish town of La Linea did not
materialize, and the couple's brief period on 'The Rock'
provided a replay in miniature of the wedding-day in London.
There was red, white and blue everywhere, and almost the
entire population of Gibraltar turned out in welcome, cheering,
waving flags, singing the National Anthem. Some Gibraltarians
saw it also as an excellent opportunity to reinforce their claim
that they should remain British. 'WELCOME HOME TO
BRITISH GIBRALTAR' ran the wording on one large banner.
'British for ever,' chanted sections of the crowd, while others, to

the tune of 'O Mr Porter', sang a song which went something like this:

> O King Juan Carlos, what can you do?
> You want something that doesn't belong to you.

The Governor, Sir William Jackson, and his wife were waiting to greet the couple when their aircraft touched down. Ships anchored in the bay tooted a welcome as Diana was presented with a bouquet of lilies and freesia. One of the few open sportscars on the Rock, borrowed for the occasion from a member of the Italian consulate, flew the Prince's personal standard as the newlyweds journeyed the winding 1½ miles from airport to dockyard. His personal standard was broken again from the mainmast of *Britannia* as the two of them went aboard. With the band of the Royal Marines playing 'I Am Sailing', as many as two hundred small craft still noisily tooting their sirens and the new Princess of Wales waving happily to those on the quayside, the royal yacht set off on its honeymoon cruise.

And that, despite elaborate searches by sea and air mounted at enormous expense by newspapers and magazines eager to get pictures of the newlyweds on honeymoon, was almost the last that was seen of *Britannia* for the next seven days. And, indeed, almost the last that was seen of Charles and Diana even by most of those aboard the royal yacht. Not even members of the crew glimpsed them as they relaxed together in the sealed-off area around the swimming-pool, and the only photographs to come out of it all were those for their private album.

Charles and Diana were not the first pair of royal newlyweds to use the yacht as a honeymoon hotel. Princess Anne and Mark Phillips had honeymooned aboard previously, and Princess Margaret and her now divorced husband, Lord Snowdon, before that. As a honeymoon sanctuary, it affords both privacy and luxury. It is about as much like an ordinary yacht as Buckingham Palace is like an ordinary house. A cruise liner all to yourself is more the picture. Meals are prepared by a chef. The dining-room can also be used as a private cinema. A Land Rover can be ferried ashore on an inflatable raft for picnics. Members of the crew tiptoe around in plimsolls so as not to disturb royal slumbers, and the portholes of the royal apartments—it would be an insult to class them merely as 'cabins'—are set two feet higher than normal so that no one can peep in. About the only disadvantage, from the point of view of a successful honeymoon, is that there are normally only single beds aboard. However, Charles had foreseen the problem and had arranged for a double bed for himself and his bride.

The new Princess of Wales did not seem to mind at all that she was almost the only woman aboard. She had no lady-in-waiting with her; none had yet been appointed. There was only a maid to wash and press her clothes. Evelyn Dagley had been one among many housemaids at Buckingham Palace until Diana, not yet a married Princess, began chatting with her as she changed the bed-linen, took a liking to her and arranged for her to become her personal maid. Princess and maid apart, everyone else aboard *Britannia* was male—the Prince himself, 12 of his staff, 22 ship's officers headed by a rear admiral and something in excess of 250 crewmen—and a Royal Marines' band of 26 musicians.

To ensure the Prince and his new Princess the privacy essential to an idyllic honeymoon, those in charge of the royal yacht indulged in a complicated game of hide-and-seek with the hordes of pressmen vainly scouring the Mediterranean by land, sea and air. To avoid revealing its whereabouts as it sailed east, signals to and from the yacht were kept to an essential minimum. One incoming call was from a motor cruiser which seemed to have lost its bearings off the coast of Sardinia. If Mahomet could not find the mountain, was it perhaps a trick devised by wily pressmen to lure the mountain to Mahomet, some of those aboard *Britannia* wondered. However, the distress call proved to be genuine, and the royal yacht and its escorting frigate *Amazon* diverted to the rescue.

Charles and Diana had originally planned to go ashore on Sardinia and see something of the island. That idea was quickly abandoned once they learned that photographers and reporters had guessed their intention and were lying in wait for them. Instead, *Britannia* sailed on into the Ionian Sea. It was ideal cruising weather, with the temperature mostly in the low seventies and the Mediterranean as calm as the proverbial millpond. Long hours of sunshine saw Charles relaxing round the yacht's swimming-pool in a pair of shorts while Diana sunbathed in a bikini. In the Ionian Sea they passed the Italian frigate *Sagittario*, its crew lining the deck, cheering and waving caps. The honeymooners waved back. They managed to slip briefly ashore on the tiny island of Ithaca, where the Prince swam in the sea from a secluded beach while the Princess, who prefers a pool to the sea, contented herself with sunbathing. While on Ithaca they also visited the villa of Constantine Gratsos, honorary president of the Onassis shipping line, but a further plan to tour the island had to be hastily abandoned because newspapermen had finally managed to locate their whereabouts. Police launches and a Greek naval gunboat circled the yacht, forcing photographers' boats to keep their distance, as it set sail again.

Back home, while the newlyweds were on honeymoon, it seemed as though the excitement over their wedding would never end. The BBC's royal wedding album sold a hundred thousand copies in the first twelve days of release, ousting Cliff Richard's 'Love Songs' from top spot in the LP charts. People queued for hours outside St James's Palace to see a selection of the 11,000 wedding gifts the couple had received. The gifts ranged from handmade tea-cosies to valuable porcelain, from cooking-pots to antique furniture, from a Rubik cube to silver tableware, from domestic items such as an omelette pan and a vacuum cleaner to jewels which, if not priceless, were very nearly so, among them a set of sapphire and diamond jewellery for the bride from the Crown Prince of Saudi Arabia. There was a Raoul Dufy painting from President Mitterand of France, a silver tea-set from Queen Ingrid of Denmark, a set of twenty silver plates from Australia, and a silver-gilt salver decorated with the Prince of Wales feathers from South Africa. Even the King and Queen of Spain, though they did not attend the wedding, sent a set of leather suitcases. Among the more touching items were a wicker-seated stool woven by a blind nun, and a grandmother clock carved by a disabled Londoner. For Charles there was a model of the minehunter *Bronington*, which he had briefly commanded in his naval days, from members of the crew; for Diana a collage made by the children of the kindergarten school where she once taught dancing and painting. Some people even anticipated the birth of a baby with gifts of dolls, teddy bears and a cuddly, hand-knitted camel.

Some 200,000 people saw the gifts while they were on display at St James's Palace. But security precautions, in particular, resulted in high expenses, and the organizers breathed a sign of relief at a final profit of £85,000 for the Royal Wedding Fund in aid of the handicapped and disabled, with more to come later when the display went on tour. The sale of official wedding programmes and souvenirs, recording and photographic royalties, television appeals and private donations swelled the fund to its final total of close on £1 million, which in the months to come was to be disbursed in grants ranging from £25 to £30,000. Prince Charles, on his return from honeymoon, personally took over the supervision of grants in excess of £2,000, and it was at his request that a major grant went to the Multiple Sclerosis Society to provide much-needed new equipment at the London Hospital and the Royal Victoria Hospital in Belfast. In addition, he and Diana asked the Royal Canadian Legion to donate the $227,000 it had raised as a wedding gift towards the setting-up of the Terry Fox Youth Centre in Ottawa.

From *Britannia*, as it headed now towards Egypt, the honeymooners sent a message of thanks to the Greek Prime Minister: 'We will always look back on our honeymoon in Greek waters with the greatest of happiness.' They had hoped to thank him personally, but, reluctantly, he was unable to accept their invitation to dine with them aboard the royal yacht. They stood together on the bridge, the Princess in Bermuda shorts and a white blouse, as *Britannia* arrived at Port Said. News of their coming had preceded them so that they sailed in with an escort of inquisitive small craft. Waiting on the quayside to greet them was a crowd of several hundred people and the local police band, playing in competition with the Royal Marines' band aboard *Britannia*. Formal greetings were extended by the British Ambassador and his wife, Sir Michael and Lady Weir, and by the Governor of Port Said, who presented Charles with the key to the city and Diana with an inscribed silver box.

That evening the royal launch was sent to Port Fouad, on the opposite bank of the Suez Canal, to collect President Sadat and his wife. The two couples spent a pleasant evening together, dining on lamb, fish and fruit, watching a fireworks display which the President had arranged on shore and the beating of retreat by the Royal Marines on the deck of the yacht, with no inkling that in a matter of weeks Sadat would be murdered as brutally and unexpectedly as Mountbatten had been. In a spontaneous gesture which was fast becoming her hallmark,

there were farewell kisses for the President and his wife from the
Princess when they took their leave.

From Port Said the honeymoon cruise headed south through
the Suez Canal and into the Red Sea. Leaving *Britannia* to
continue on the long journey to Australia, there to await the
arrival of the Queen and Prince Philip, the newlyweds went
ashore to a desert airfield where an RAF aircraft was waiting to
fly them back to Britain.

They touched down at Lossiemouth in Scotland looking
tanned, relaxed and very much in love, the Princess with her fair
hair bleached several shades lighter from long hours of
sunbathing. To the delight of Air Force wives and children
waiting to catch a glimpse of them, they did not drive off
immediately but went walkabout. The wedding-day apart, that
impromptu walkabout constituted Diana's first public function
in Britain as a princess. There was another to follow. Instead of
driving direct to Balmoral, the Royal Family's Scottish retreat,
they detoured through the neighbouring town of Lossiemouth
so that people there might have an opportunity to see them.

They arrived at Balmoral, some eighty miles away, just too
late to see Anne and Mark. Charles' sister and her husband had
already left for some equestrian trials in Derbyshire before
returning to their home at Gatcombe Park. But others of the
family were still there, and the newlyweds came in for some
good-natured teasing from Prince Philip and Charles' brother
Andrew. The honeymoon had been 'fabulous', Diana assured
them.

The relaxed holiday atmosphere of Balmoral, its rear
entrance constantly littered with fishing-rods and muddy
wellies, afforded exactly the right setting for the young new
Princess of Wales and her royal in-laws to become better
acquainted. In a sense, of course, Diana has known the Royal
Family all her life. The Queen is godmother to her brother, and
she herself had been to parties with Andrew and Edward in
childhood. But now a closer, more intimate relationship had to
be forged. Balmoral also provided an excellent opportunity for
easing her gently, step by step, into the new and infinitely more
public way of life which now lay ahead of her. A start was made
that first Sunday when she attended morning service in nearby
Crathie with her husband, his parents and brothers. The crowd
lining the quarter-mile route was the largest ever seen there, an

early indication of the quite astonishing effect the new Princess was to have on royal public life.

In the run-up to their wedding not all had been sweetness and light between the newlyweds and the Press. Charles had been more amused perhaps than annoyed when Diana, very shortly after their relationship became public property, was persuaded to pose for a photograph which, if it fell a good deal short of what has become known as a 'page three study', was nevertheless a little too revealing for a future Princess of Wales. 'I thought you had good legs, but did you have to show them to the world?' he is said to have teased her. But he was very angry indeed over the story of their supposed late-night meeting aboard the royal train. So too was his mother. And Diana herself was extremely upset by an interview quoting what were said to be her views on marriage. In light of all this, it is perhaps not to be wondered at that Charles, at Sandringham a few days before he finally braced himself to propose, told a batch of assembled newsmen, 'I wish you all a happy new year and your editors a particularly nasty one.'

But now, in the after-glow of their Mediterranean honeymoon, all was forgotten and forgiven. At least, for the moment. In the hope of being permitted to enjoy the remainder of their stay at Balmoral in peace, the Prince and Princess, four days after arriving there, agreed to a photo call and Press conference. Television cameras whirred and still cameras clicked non-stop as they appeared together near the Brig O' Dee, not far from Braemar, with the peak which was the setting for the Prince's children's story, *The Old Man Of Lochnagar*, providing a backdrop to the scene. Charles was wearing a kilt of the Gordon Highlanders, one of several regiments of which he is Colonel-in-Chief, while Diana wore an outfit of dog-tooth design with a kick-pleat skirt and blouson jacket.

She cuddled close to Charles in a manner that was not simply for the benefit of the cameras, enthused by it though the cameramen were. It was, in the main, a relaxed and jokey occasion. 'A very happy Christmas to you all,' Charles greeted the assembled reporters and photographers, a joke that was not immediately understood by everyone. Scotland was 'about forty degrees cooler' than the Red Sea, he explained. A slightly more nervous Diana was perhaps less forthcoming. How was the honeymoon? 'Fabulous.' How was she enjoying married life? 'I can highly recommend it,' she said, almost echoing the words used by her royal mother-in-law at the time of her silver wedding anniversary. Tongue in cheek, Charles expressed the hope that the newspapermen had enjoyed themselves chasing around the Mediterranean in search of the honeymooners. It had been rather an expensive chase, one of them told him. 'Good,' said the Prince. And even Diana could not resist a small teasing dig when, as a gesture of thanks at the end of the Press conference, she was presented with a bouquet. 'Which of you put it on your expenses?' she wanted to know.

The Royal Family's holiday in Scotland that year followed the traditional pattern established as far back as Queen Victoria's day: fishing, shooting, picnics amidst the heather or along the edge of Loch Muick (though picnic meals these days include food cooked on a portable barbecue). The only public appearances were the morning services at Crathie on Sundays and a visit to the Highland Games at Braemar, with Charles sporting a kilt and Diana dressed in a tartan two-piece with a black velvet tam-o'-shanter. The so-called Gillies' Balls, held in the castle ballroom, permitted her to display her aptitude for Scottish dancing. Her propensity for the sporting life beloved by her husband and his family was perhaps less obvious, though she did her best to conform. She started horse-riding again, the first time she had done so since her pony bolted and she was thrown at the age of nine. She went salmon fishing with Prince Charles and accompanied him onto the grouse moors and when he went stalking—until a single rifle shot chipped, though it did not shatter, the growing love affair between Princess and public.

What actually happened was, and still is, cloaked in mystery. There were so many different rumours and some somewhat conflicting official statements. The most lurid rumour was that the Princess had shot and wounded a red deer which had later been finished off by someone else. Not so, said an official statement. She had been stalking but had not shot a stag 'on this occasion'. Which immediately raised the question, of course, as to whether she had done so on a previous occasion. Later the official statement was changed. Now it was that 'Yes, the Princess had been stalking,' but 'No, it was not known that she had actually shot anything.' Whatever had actually happened, the League Against Cruel Sports promptly criticized the Princess for joining what it labelled 'the killing-for-fun brigade'.

Among the public, women more than men were distressed at this apparent flaw in the image of their new idol. 'How could she?' they asked each other in supermarkets and bingo halls. Not all, of course. Countrywomen, with their more realistic outlook, saw the culling of a stag as no more reprehensible than the slaughter of a pig or the killing of a chicken. And in Scotland, where stalking and the sale of venison are big business, adding something like £3 million a year to the country's economy, there were more shrugs than criticism. Overall, as a public opinion poll revealed, 52 per cent of people disapproved of the Princess taking up stalking, 24 per cent approved and a further 24 per cent had no firm view on the matter. Diana herself, a friend said, was very upset by the whole affair.

With the departure of the rest of the Royal Family, the Queen and Prince Philip to prepare for their forthcoming tours of Australia and New Zealand, the newlyweds were again alone (except for the servants, of course). Balmoral, with its dozens of rooms, seemed too large and impersonal for just the two of them, and they decided to move into the smaller, more intimate surroundings of Craigowen, a lodge on the estate. With fewer distractions now that the rest of the family had left, Diana settled down to learn some phrases in Welsh in readiness for their coming tour of Wales. It would be her first major engagement as a princess and if she viewed it with some degree of apprehension, that was surely understandable. Apart from that tour of Wales, almost obligatory on the newlyweds in their roles as Prince and Princess of Wales, it was planned that she should ease herself into her new life with a 'gentle' series of public engagements, mostly with her husband along in support, but with a few solo sorties too. Then the peace and quiet of Craigowen was abruptly shattered by the shocking news from Egypt.

There had been, earlier, news from London which had seemed bad enough at the time, the vandalism of the portrait of the Princess on display at the National Portrait Gallery. Intended as a companion piece to an earlier painting of Prince Charles, the portrait had been painted by Bryan Organ shortly before the wedding, depicting the Princess in a trendy outfit of trousers and waistcoat. While Charles and Diana had both expressed themselves 'delighted' with it, not everyone was impressed by its pop-art image, though it was not dislike of its art form which caused a twenty-year-old student to slash it with a knife before tearing at it with his hands. He did it, it was stated when he was later sentenced to six months' imprisonment for criminal damage, to draw attention to social deprivation in Northern Ireland. Badly damaged though the portrait was, it was not beyond restoration, fortunately. Perhaps only an art expert could have spotted the difference when it was later returned to its place in the Gallery following long hours of intricate work by a restorer and a re-toucher. 'A fantastic piece of work,' Bryan Organ said by way of congratulation. To safeguard the portrait against possible future vandalism, it was given a Perspex shield, with similar protective treatment afforded to the matching portrait of Prince Charles and the Gallery's Annigoni portrait of the Queen.

All the Royal Family had been upset by the news that the portrait had been vandalized, Diana especially. But a portrait is an inanimate object, and the further news she and Charles were to receive after the rest of the family had left was to see them both far more shocked. It must have seemed to them almost as though Balmoral was destined to be the place where they received bad news. Two years before, at the very beginning of their relationship, it had been news of Earl Mountbatten's murder in Ireland. Now their enjoyment of what was tantamount to a second honeymoon was destroyed by news of the assassination of President Sadat, with whom they had shared such a pleasant evening on the royal yacht towards the end of their honeymoon cruise only a few weeks previously. Upset and distressed as they both were, Charles decided that he must fly to Egypt to attend the President's funeral. Diana would go with him, she said. But the risk—the same risk of possible assassination which kept America's President Reagan from attending the funeral—was deemed too great for her to make the trip. Indeed, there were some among those whose duty it is to advise the Royal Family on such matters who would have preferred it if Prince Charles had not gone. But he was insistent on attending the funeral, though he saw the wisdom of prevailing upon his wife to remain behind.

Their goodbyes were said in private, and only they know whether or not Diana wept at parting, as she did publicly in their betrothal days when he left her to visit America. She both missed him and worried for him while he was in Cairo—so much so that she could not remain patiently at Balmoral but flew to

London where she sat on the airport in an Andover of the Queen's Flight to await his return and welcome him back.

With Highgrove, their new home in Gloucestershire, still in the process of renovation and not yet ready for occupation, Charles and Diana stayed on at Balmoral until well into October, enjoying the privacy and intimacy of being alone together. The occasional royal chore interrupted their idyll. Charles journeyed south on one occasion to visit the Toxteth district of Liverpool, which not long before had been the scene of violent rioting. Prior to his arrival, police dogs were used to check for explosives in the youth club he was to visit and, during his visit, police reserves remained discreetly out of sight in side streets while he inspected the club, which had earlier received £150 from the Prince's Trust Fund to launch its own magazine. In the event, the occasion passed off without incident other than that Charles found himself presented with a mahogany trolley as a belated wedding gift. He also visited the Handsworth district of Birmingham where two young Rastafarians thanked him for the £300, also from the Trust Fund, which had provided equipment for a photographic dark-room.

Diana did not accompany him to Liverpool and Birmingham. In his absence from their Balmoral hideaway, she flew to London to sort out some of the furnishings which would be needed at Highgrove and also took the opportunity of re-visiting the kindergarten where she had taught not long before, chatting with the children, as well as with her old friend Kay Seth-Smith, and thanking them for the collage they had made as a wedding gift. While in London she also did what was officially described as 'some shopping'.

She flew back to Aberdeen on the British Airways shuttle, travelling in the company of her personal detective as 'Mr and Mrs Smith'. The detective's name really was Smith—Police Inspector Graham Smith. Pseudonymous travel is a well-established royal custom, dating back at least to Queen Victoria's day. She called herself the Countess of Balmoral when visiting relatives in Europe. The Duke of Windsor, when he was briefly King Edward VIII, styled himself Duke of Lancaster when abroad in the company of Mrs Simpson. Prince Charles has employed several pseudonyms in his time—Perkins (the name of his former private detective), Chester (Earl of Chester being one of his lesser titles) and Renfrew (another of his lesser titles). It was as Charles Renfrew that he sometimes telephoned Diana and dated her in their courtship days.

Such ploys seldom work completely and did not in Diana's case. Airport workers and fellow passengers aboard the shuttle recognized her immediately. But it worked sufficiently to prevent any enterprising reporter or photographer from sitting close to her.

Even if she did not show it, she must have been filled with excitement as she flew north again to Aberdeen. A gossip columnist, writing next day about her visit to her old kindergarten, pondered the question of when she would have a child of her own. 'Not before next autumn,' he predicted. He was wrong. The shopping excursion in which Diana was said to have indulged during that visit to London had actually been an appointment with the royal gynaecologist, George Pinker. As a result of that appointment, she was returning to Balmoral—and reunion with her husband—with the joyful news that already, after less than three months of marriage, she was expecting their first baby.

3 Welcome to Wales

Though the fact that there was a baby on the way was still the couple's close-kept secret when they toured Wales at the end of October 1981, pregnancy was already endowing Diana with a fresh bloom of beauty. And the pangs of morning sickness, because she was still less than two months pregnant, were not yet afflicting her to any extent (though they would do so later). It was as well that she did not suffer from morning sickness, for a royal tour can be arduous enough without that, and certainly for anyone, like Diana, who joins them for the first time. Yet her very inexperience may have proved an asset on that tour of Wales. New and novel as everything was, she reacted with all her youthful zest and enthusiasm.

Two qualities have long been demanded of those who tour with the royal roadshow, female stars in particular—endless charm and boundless endurance. To these, in more recent years, had been added a third essential—courage. If presidents are perhaps more likely to be assassination targets than princes or princesses, the possibility remains, as the murder of Earl Mountbatten has shown.

On her first-ever royal tour, which was also her first-ever visit to Wales, the new young Princess of Wales showed that she was endowed with all three essential qualities. She endured cold winds and icy showers as well as angry chanting and the discharge of stink-bombs from the few not prepared to accept the English-born Charles as Prince of Wales. She charmed Welsh loyalists—and they were in overwhelming majority—with the naturalness of her personality and the warmth of her smile. Disdaining to wear gloves on walkabouts, her hands were frequently bruised, grazed or scratched by the enthusiastic and exuberant Welsh. Presumably her husband had warned her what would happen. So frequently and so heartily had his hand been shaken on an earlier tour of Wales that at the end of it all he had had to have medical treatment for his right shoulder. But if the Welsh crowds, excited at having in their midst the first Princess of Wales for more than seventy years, were even more demonstrative than the Welsh always are, Diana was hardly less so. Responding eagerly to the excitement surrounding her, sometimes she stretched out both hands at once for people to grasp and ended up almost tugged off her feet. If the possibility that in the course of the tour she might encounter something more lethal than stink-bombs ever entered her head, she let it deter her no more than the inclement weather. Perhaps her husband had talked to her about that too. 'If you are going to worry about that sort of thing, you might as well give up,' is the Prince's attitude.

With the IRA again managing to plant a few of their bombs in London itself, their Welsh counterparts saw it as a time to flex their own muscles. Their first move was a fire-bomb in the army recruiting office at Pontypridd—'a particularly nasty device', according to the head of the South Wales CID. However, adequate warning was given, and an army bomb squad succeeded in defusing the bomb safely. This was before the start of the couple's tour, and one result was a decision to change the proposed route so as to bypass the Welshest part of Wales, an area centred on Aberystwyth, where Charles had spent a few weeks at the University of Wales immediately preceding his investiture and where there had been noisy demonstrations when he revisited the area only the year before. If it was a necessary omission, dictated by the circumstances of the moment, it was also one which disappointed thousands of Welsh loyalists in Aberystwyth who had been looking forward to catching their first live glimpse of the Prince's bride. Then, after the tour had actually started, news that a group of self-confessed anarchists had set up camp in a lay-by at Haverfordwest brought another last-minute change of route, with the royal train making a fifty-mile detour to avoid going anywhere near them. Royal security, always tight, was tightened more than ever. Members of the Special Branch moved from town to town ahead of the royal couple in an attempt to sniff out trouble-makers and nip possible plots in the bud. Each night, at the end of a full and tiring day of seeing and being seen, Charles and Diana slept aboard the royal train, where they could be most easily protected. There were other security precautions too, but

these, for fairly obvious reasons, were kept as secret as the
overnight locations of their mobile sleeping-quarters.

As the tour ran its course, there were several incidents which
might have unnerved a less resolute couple. Another fire-bomb
was planted, this time in Cardiff, which the couple would visit at
the end of their tour. There was noisy chanting here and there,
smoke-bombs were set off, aerosol paint was sprayed on the
royal Rolls Royce by a woman member of the Welsh Language
Society, and a threatening note was sent by a group styling
themselves 'Sons of Glyndwr'. 'We will not forget 1969,' said the
note, which was written in Welsh. 'Beware Caernarvon.' It was
taken to be a reference to the fact that, at the time of the Prince's
investiture, two would-be bombers had blown themselves up
with their own bomb while trying to plant it in the path of the
royal train.

If the royal couple were at all unnerved by all this, and by the
tight security to which they were subject in consequence, they
gave little outward sign of it. The Prince's very natural concern
for his wife may have resulted in his looking a little grim upon
occasion but the Princess was never less than her smiling,
cheerful self. Certainly neither of them ever wavered. Their
security advisers would have preferred them not to have
appeared in public on that same balcony of Caernarvon Castle
where the Queen, twelve years before, had presented 'My most
dear son' to the Welsh people following his investiture as Prince
of Wales. They did it just the same, and the fact that Diana's
smile faded momentarily as she stood beside her husband on the
balcony had nothing to do with lack of courage. She was
concerned that the strong wind blowing at the time might whip
off her hat and play havoc with her hair-style.

If all this tends to give the impression that they found Wales a
sea of trouble rather than a land of song, such was far from
being the case. Unpleasant incidents were the work of small
extremist minorities. The overwhelming majority of the Welsh
people welcomed the couple, the new Princess of Wales in
particular, with heart-warming and noisy enthusiasm, surging
forward during walkabouts to talk to her, touch her, heaping
her with flowers.

Over the three days of the tour the royal couple covered a
total of four hundred miles, starting with the unemployment
blackspot of Shotton, where out-of-work teenagers had spruced

up the railway station specially for the occasion, and ending in Cardiff, where the Princess, if she had not yet learned sufficient Welsh to join in the singing of the national anthem, still managed to express her thanks partly in Welsh when presented with the Freedom of the City. Translated, what she said was, 'How proud I am to be Princess of such a wonderful place and of the Welsh people, who are very special to me.'

Despite the warning to 'Beware Caernarvon', the only untoward incident there was a little paint sprayed on the royal car. They were welcomed there by Princess Margaret's ex-husband, Lord Snowdon, in his role as Constable of Caernarvon Castle. Diana returned his greeting with a kiss before being escorted inside to sit with Charles in freezing wind on an open-air slate podium while a children's choir sang to them in Welsh. Unlike the Prince's investiture, which cost the taxpayer something of the order of £200,000, his 1981 return visit to Caernarvon did not cost anyone a penny. Or so Lord Snowdon insisted, though perhaps not quite accurately. All those extra police on duty had to be paid for somewhere along the line. Still, as royal visits go, it was not expensive, and those who managed to see the Princess considered it money well spent.

At Bangor, their last stopping-place on the first day—they had previously visited Rhyl and Llandudno as well as Shotton and Caernarvon—there were moments of unease when demonstrators, opposed to the Prince's appointment as Chancellor of the University of Wales, shook the metal barriers forming the walkabout route so violently that they threatened to give way. Charles quickly shepherded his wife to a safer spot while their bodyguards closed around them, and police moved into the crowd to arrest the trouble-makers. There was also another briefly apprehensive moment of which the Princess seemed blithely unaware. Amidst all the bouquets and posies being thrust upon her, a man in the crowd held out a string bag containing two round greyish-white objects. Without thinking, she took it, then passed it to Prince Charles. 'These must be for you, darling,' she said. Charles peered at the contents of the bag. 'What are they?' he asked. That he was aware of the possibility of danger, even if his wife was not, showed in the quip he made when told that the greyish-white objects were nothing more lethal than turnips: 'Not the exploding kind, I hope.'

If Day 1 of the tour was marred by biting wind, Day 2 saw

them caught in such a downpour of rain that the ostrich feathers on Diana's hat sagged until they were almost non-existent. But nothing seemed to dampen her spirits as she trudged around sheltered by an umbrella, though she admitted at one point, 'My feet are freezing.' Charles delivered his usual quota of princely jokes, saying that it was one of those days when he was glad he was no longer at sea, and asking one group of people, 'Are you all going to the pub after this for a stiff drink?' Husbandly concern showed again in Haverfordwest as Diana paused in pelting rain to chat with people in the crowd. 'Darling, don't walk out in the rain,' he urged her, slipping an affectionate arm about her waist. 'You'll get so wet.' Then, as Diana went on chatting, getting wetter by the minute, he took over the umbrella held by her lady-in-waiting and held it over her himself.

If there were those among her royal in-laws who had perhaps read too much into that pre-marital incident when Diana fled a polo ground in tears and feared that she might be unable to cope with the stress and strain of the royal round, that three-day tour of Wales quickly and happily put them right. Whatever was asked of her, officially or otherwise, she responded as to the palace born. Enthusiastic beginner though she may have been, rather than a fully fledged professional princess, she more than lived up to her schoolgirl reputation of being 'the girl who tried hardest'. And not only tried, but succeeded triumphantly. 'She has coped extremely well,' said one experienced member of the royal entourage at the end of it all. A Welsh woman put it more poetically: 'She's the flower in the royal forest.'

Some of her success, of course, stemmed from shrewd advice, as witness the delight of the Welsh when she appeared on the first day of the tour in a striking outfit of red and green, the Welsh national colours. But much more was due to her own natural qualities of warmth, enthusiasm and good humour. Prior exposure to the crowds at Royal Ascot and to the guests at a Buckingham Palace garden party may also have contributed towards the success she enjoyed in Wales, but to only a small degree. Those occasions had, after all, been very different. At Ascot she had been remote from the crowd, displayed in a royal landau and cocooned in the royal box. The hand-picked guests at the palace garden party had been too restrained to do more than politely clap her appearance. But there was nothing either remote or restrained about the crowds in Wales. They pressed in upon her, called her by name, clutched her, tugged her, kissed her hand. It was as though they saw her as some tribal fetish whose very touch would ward off evil. She responded to it all magnificently, allowing herself to be tugged, clutched, hand-kissed. She accepted posies from the sometimes grubby hands of small children with the same show of delight as she displayed when presented with elaborate bouquets on more formal occasions. People tried all manner of tricks to catch her eye and attract her attention. 'My name is Diana too,' proclaimed a placard held by one toddler. It worked. The Princess stopped to talk to her. Even the hovering close presence of reporters and photographers no longer unnerved her, it seemed, and she had the occasional word of greeting for those she recognized among the accompanying pressmen.

Again and again a fleeting resemblance to the Queen Mother showed through, and not only in her seeming fondness for ostrich feathers. In her spontaneity, too. More easily than the Queen, she seemed able to indulge in the small-talk which is the staple diet of royal walkabouts. Not once was there any occasion for Charles to intervene because she had dried up in conversation or to encourage her with a whispered aside of 'Buck up, sweetheart,' as Prince Philip sometimes did with the Queen in the early years of her reign. Diana seemed to have the right word, or very nearly the right word, for everyone she spoke to. 'I've got a miniature of you,' she told a small girl dressed in traditional Welsh costume, showing her a Welsh doll she had been given shortly before. 'What nice shiny medals,' she congratulated an old soldier. Nor did she forget his wife. 'Did you polish them for him?' she asked. If such remarks, reproduced in print, seem perhaps trite and uninspired, they sound very different to those to whom they are actually addressed. To them, they become treasured memories to be carefully stored away and recalled with infinite pleasure from time to time in the years to come.

It was perhaps inevitable that Diana should slip up occasionally. In Llandudno, where she and Charles were each presented with a small silver bowl, she was seen to turn hers over and study the under-side. Some thought she was looking to see if the bowl was hallmarked or not. If she was, it was perhaps a very small departure from accepted royal behaviour. But the day she no longer makes the occasional small slip will be a sad one. Her naturalness will be gone.

The pair of silver bowls was among several official gifts the couple received during their three days in Wales. In St David's they were given a water-colour of the cathedral by local artist John Rogers. Carmarthen gave them a commemorative plate, while a visit to the Royal Welsh Show resulted in the gift of a Welsh heifer and a yearling ewe. On a more humble level, it seemed that everyone, everywhere, wanted to give the Princess something, flowers mostly, but also Welsh dolls, verses, children's drawings, even sticks of rock. It was fortunate that the Welsh phrases she had learned included the one for 'Thank you'. She said it again and again and again.

Her poor husband found himself rather left out of it all. Those who found themselves on the 'wrong side' of a royal walkabout had no alternative but to give their flowers to Charles while making it clear that they were not actually for him. They were for 'Princess Diana'. He took it in good part. 'I'm just a collector of flowers these days,' he joked. Later, when that particular joke became a trifle worn, he changed the words if not the tune: 'I'm getting very good at collecting flowers for my wife.' Diana herself was sometimes so heaped with flowers that she was forced to pass them on to her newly appointed lady-in-waiting and others in the royal entourage. Even policewomen, a burly police sergeant and, on one occasion, a rather embarrassed Nicholas Edwards, the Welsh Secretary, found themselves pressed into service as flower-carriers.

Buckingham Palace might ordain that, as a princess by marriage rather than birth, the latest member of the Royal Family should be addressed as Princess of Wales rather than Princess Diana, but the Welsh crowds could not be bothered with such niceties. Even 'Princess', it seemed, was a little too formal for some of them. 'Over here, Diana,' they would call. 'Over here.' And at Pontypridd, where some twenty thousand people crowded the streets to see the royal couple, Diana became Di, a pet-name which even her own family do not use. But the Welsh people, that day, felt themselves closer than family. 'Di, Di, Di—We want Di,' they chanted over and over again.

Usually, on walkabouts, the couple would separate, Charles taking one side of the route and Diana the other. Inevitably, the result was delighted enthusiasm among the crowd who found themselves on the 'right side', that being the side of the walkabout favoured by the Princess, and a degree of not always well-concealed disappointment on the other. Charles noticed, of course. It was impossible for him not to have done so. For perhaps the first time since graduating into public life, he found himself being upstaged and thoroughly enjoyed the experience, proud and pleased by his wife's obvious popularity. On one occasion, aware of the disappointed atmosphere on his side of the walkabout, he called Diana over. As a result, smiles immediately changed to glumness on the side she had left. Elsewhere, he made a joke of it. 'Sorry I haven't got enough wives to go round,' he professed to apologize. On another occasion it was, 'Sorry that I've only one of her and she's over there.' And in Brecon it became, 'Sorry, but you'll have to make do with me.'

Royal wit can sometimes be misunderstood, of course. Perhaps it was the thought that he would soon be a father which caused Charles, when he was presented with a miniature Welsh coracle in Carmarthen, to joke that it would be 'very nice in the bath'. Perhaps it was baby's bath-time he had in mind. But with no one except himself and his wife (and of course the royal gynaecologist) yet aware that there was a baby on the way, the joke fell embarrassingly flat.

It was while visiting Llwynypia Hospital that the royal parents-to-be came close to giving away their secret. 'Babies!' Diana almost squealed the word as she pushed passed everyone else in her eagerness to inspect the maternity ward. Their schedule for the visit provided that, while the Princess was in the maternity ward, Charles would inspect other parts of the hospital. Instead of doing so, he followed her in. Together, they stood chatting to twenty-one-year-old Shirley Bowen, whose baby daughter, Lilian, had been born only a matter of hours before, both eager to know more of the mystery of childbirth. Diana was particularly concerned to find out how long Mrs Bowen had been in labour. Eight hours, she was told. Even when Diana moved on to talk to someone else, Charles remained behind, desirous of knowing more.

'Was your husband with you when your baby was born?' he asked.

'Yes,' said Mrs Bowen. 'He was.'

Charles' brother-in-law, Mark Phillips, had been with Princess Anne for the birth of each of their two babies, and now Charles nodded at Mrs Bowen's answer. 'I think that is a very good thing,' he said.

If royal behaviour so far had not let the baby out of the bag, another small incident surely did. Mothers whose babies are born in the Llwynypia maternity wing are presented with a stork-and-baby medallion to commemorate the event. Charles spotted a medallion, picked it up, turned it over and showed it to his wife. 'We mustn't go home without one of these,' he said to her.

Nurses who heard him looked quickly at Diana, then at each other. 'I think the Princess is expecting,' one whispered to the rest. 'Her face has the bloom of motherhood.'

4 Settling In

The baby the Princess was expecting was still a secret she shared only with her husband and her gynaecologist. A sharp-eyed maternity nurse in Wales may have formed a shrewd idea as to her condition, but she could not actually *know*. No one could, and the rumours which continually surfaced were the result of wishful thinking rather than anything else. Such rumours were by no means confined to Britain. People everywhere were fascinated by this girl who had won the heart of the Prince of Wales.

The Queen, half-a-world away, was asked pointblank about one such rumour as she toured New Zealand. Was it true, Sir Graham Latimer, chairman of the Maori Council, wanted to know, that her daughter-in-law was expecting a baby? 'If not,' joked Sir Graham, 'we suggest you tell Prince Charles to get on with it.'

The Queen could hardly have been expected to answer such a direct question, put to her in public, even if she had known the answer. As it happened, she did not yet know, however much she may have been hoping that her daughter-in-law would produce a future king in direct line as promptly as she had done herself. It was not until the Queen returned from her tour of Australia, New Zealand and other places besides that Charles and Diana let her and Prince Philip into the secret. Both were 'delighted', they said. So were Diana's divorced parents when she told them a little later. 'That's great news,' her mother, the Hon. Mrs Shand-Kydd, told her over the telephone from her home in Scotland. 'I'm absolutely thrilled,' said her father. 'Diana wants this baby very much,' he confided. 'She will make a wonderful mother.' Brothers and sisters on both sides of the family were equally let into the secret ahead of any official announcement. So were the three girls, Anne Bolton, Virginia Pitman and Carolyn Pride, who had shared Diana's

London flat—and the secret of courtship—in the days when she was a kindergarten teacher.

For Charles and Diana, as for any other couple of young newlyweds, those early months of marriage were a time of idyllic happiness, made all the happier by the knowledge that they would soon be parents. They delighted in each other's company. Diana, an accomplished dancer even if she had grown too tall ever to realize her schoolgirl dream of becoming a ballet dancer, tried to teach her husband to tap-dance. The lessons did not last long. 'It's too hard on my ankles,' Charles protested.

Unlike so many other young newlyweds, they had no financial problems, of course; no worry over paying a mortgage as first-time buyers, and no fear that Charles might find himself redundant as Britain struggled through its deepest recession since the 1930s. But two, even if they are the Prince and Princess of Wales, cannot live as cheaply as one. In any event, two would shortly become three, which would add to the expense of family living.

It is one of the anomalies of the British system of constitutional monarchy that the state, which hands out money on a not ungenerous scale to his parents, brothers, sister, grandmother and aunt, pays Prince Charles, as heir to throne, nothing directly for making so many public appearances and all the other work he does in the national interest. It hardly needs to, of course. As heir to the throne, he is Duke of Cornwall as well as Prince of Wales, and in his ducal capacity he is extremely wealthy in his own right. His wealth derives from the Duchy of Cornwall, an ancient parcel of royal lands set up over six centuries ago by Edward III for the benefit of his son and heir, that selfsame Black Prince whose wife was the first Princess of Wales. It has been the accepted inheritance of the heir to the throne ever since and passed into Prince Charles' three-year-old hands when the death of his grandfather, King George VI, in 1952 saw his mother succeed to the throne while he became her heir.

Today, the Duchy of Cornwall, so-called, totals around 128,000 acres scattered across seven counties, as well as the Isles of Scilly and parts of metropolitan London. Its holdings are many and varied, farms and apartment blocks, castles and woodland, and almost an entire village near Cirencester. It includes oyster beds, a granite quarry and a lead mine.

Dartmoor Prison stands on land which forms part of the Duchy. So does the Oval cricket ground in London, along with several public houses and a fish-and-chip shop.

When Charles originally inherited the Duchy on the death of his grandfather, it was producing a net income in the region of £90,000 a year, no very vast sum in today's inflationary era but substantial enough in 1952 and certainly more than was necessary for a mere three-year-old, however royal. His mother, at the same time that she surrendered her own Crown Estate holdings to the nation in exchange for an annual allowance known as the Civil List, also agreed that the bulk of her son's revenues should likewise be surrendered to the state until he came of age. By the time Charles came into his full Black Prince inheritance, the Duchy's income had more than doubled, due in part to inflation and in part to efficient management techniques and modernization of many of the properties, particularly those in London—and all of it, because Charles is heir to the throne, tax free.

As a youthful bachelor still living with his parents in their palace home, and later with a berth aboard ship during his spell in the Royal Navy, Charles hardly needed so much. Accordingly, he volunteered to surrender half his Duchy income to the Exchequer in lieu of income tax. In those days, with few financial commitments of consequence and no marital responsibilities, it still left him more than enough to get by on. But now things were different. He was a married man. He had a wife to keep as well as a baby on the way (even if the nation was not yet aware of that fact). There might well be, almost certainly would be, other babies to follow. These days, in his growing public role as Prince of Wales, he required more aides. There were the dual expenses of an apartment at Kensington Palace, two apartments knocked into one, in fact, and of a house in the country. Two homes meant two lots of servants. They had just engaged a new cook-housekeeper for Highgrove after sorting through the applications stemming from an advertisement placed in a magazine, with Diana personally interviewing the successful applicant. Soon they would have to think about hiring a nanny for the baby.

If Diana was adequately to fulfil her triple role of wife, mother and Princess of Wales, she too now required her own small team of aides. She already had the personal maid who had accompanied her on honeymoon and the full-time lady-in-waiting, Anne Beckwith-Smith, a twenty-nine-year-old bachelor girl formerly employed by Sotheby's, who was with her on the tour of Wales. There were also two part-time ladies-in-waiting, both married women, the Hon. Mrs Lavinia Baring and Mrs Hazel West, wife of Lieutenant-Colonel George West, Assistant Comptroller in the Lord Chamberlain's office. The amount of correspondence already pouring in for the Princess, the innumerable requests to go here, there and everywhere, necessitated a private secretary (the post went to Oliver Everett, formerly First Secretary at the British Embassy in Madrid) and a stenographer or two. It all meant more salaries to be paid, more expenses to be met. Then there were all the new clothes a professional princess necessarily requires; all those worn in Wales, all those which would be needed for the growing stream of future public engagements. A wife who is also required to inspect children's homes, tour factories, open hospitals, plant trees, launch ships, attend luncheons, concerts, banquets, balls, cannot be dressed on the cheap.

If Prince Charles did not have occasion actually to worry and fret over his finances, as many another young husband might have done as he contemplated the increased cost of supporting a wife and child, he nevertheless took prudent steps to re-arrange things to better advantage. For the future, he decided, the amount of his income he paid voluntarily to the Exchequer would be reduced from fifty to twenty-five per cent. Explaining the need for such reduction, a spokesman said on the Prince's behalf: 'The expenses of his Household and the amounts required to meet the cost of undertaking public duties will rise considerably. In particular, there will be the additional cost of maintaining a separate establishment at Kensington Palace and a considerable increase in the size of the Prince and Princess's Household.' As things turned out, the Prince was to benefit in another direction also. His income from the Duchy of Cornwall, which had already risen to £550,445 in his last year as a bachelor, was to rise still further over the next two years, to £771,480 in 1981 and to £795,126 in 1982. He was more fortunate than most young husbands too in that he did not have to pay for his new country house out of his own pocket. Or so it would appear. Sealed lips are normally the order of the day where matters of royal finance are concerned, but a spokesman for the Duchy of Cornwall did concede that the sale of a manor in Cullompton and two properties in the village of Daglingworth 'could be said to have funded the main house at Highgrove', with the additional sale of some agricultural cottages meeting the cost of the 347 acres which surround the house.

The actual price paid to the former owner of Highgrove, Maurice Macmillan, son of former Prime Minister Harold Macmillan, is a close-kept royal secret. At the time of the sale property experts valued the Georgian house and surrounding land at between £750,000 and £1 million. One expert's informed guess—and it can be no more than a guess, the property having been bought privately prior to auction—is that it changed hands for something in the region of £800,000.

If the purchase of Highgrove, some three or four months before Charles even proposed to Diana, served as a signal that he had marriage in mind, it was a signal which came as a considerable disappointment to the villagers of Chevening in Kent, who had hoped that he would live there when he married and settled down. Chevening, a seventeenth-century country mansion thought to have been designed by Inigo Jones, was left to the nation, along with its antique furniture and art treasures, plus a trust fund to maintain it all, on condition that the Prince of Wales was given the first choice of living there. Charles said at first that he did not want to live there, then changed his mind and moved in, then changed his mind yet again and decided upon Highgrove.

The fact that Chevening would never really be his, that he could never do with it as he wished, was perhaps a motivating factor in his decision not to make it his home on marriage. There were others. If Chevening was closer to London, Highgrove was handier for Wales, and there was a convenient RAF air-field nearby. The surrounding Gloucestershire countryside abounded with royal relatives and friends. Gatcombe Park, the country home the Queen had bought for Princess Anne and Mark Phillips, was only some eight miles away. Prince and Princess Michael of Kent, Lord Tryon and his Australian-born wife Dale, and Lieutenant-Colonel Andrew Parker-Bowles and his wife Camilla, in whose garden Charles made his first ambiguous approach to Diana on the subject of marriage, all live within easy driving distance. Most appealing of all to

Charles perhaps, if not to Diana, was the fact that the area offered so many sporting possibilities, including polo at Cirencester and hunting with the Beaufort.

Described as 'a distinguished Georgian house' when it first came onto the market, Highgrove was built in the reign of George III, the ancestor whom Prince Charles considers to be a much misunderstood monarch. Set amidst wooded parkland, a light, airy, well-proportioned structure, its front draped with wistaria and clematis, it is a good example of the architecture of the period with its wealth of panelled walls, period fireplaces and moulded ceilings. Charles and Diana moved in shortly after completing their very successful tour of Wales, and almost the first thing Diana did was to run upstairs and take a look at the three rooms which would serve as a nursery wing for the expected baby.

Redecorated throughout, its interior redesigned by Dudley Poplak (the South African who also designed their Kensington Palace apartment for them), the kitchen remodelled, its furnishings including the specially made bed which was a wedding gift from the Foreign Diplomatic Corps, other gifts dotted here and there, the house now presented a very different aspect from when Charles had first taken Diana to see it shortly before their wedding. On that occasion it had been bare of furniture still, lacking carpets and curtains. Downstairs only one room had been finished. Elsewhere, carpenters and decorators were still at work. Now the workmen had gone. About all that remained to be done was the installation of the new wrought-iron gates being made by metalwork teacher Hector Cole as a wedding gift from the people of nearby Tetbury. The drawing-room, with its marble fireplace, looked comfortable as well as elegant. Library and study were equally pleasing, while the dining-room afforded a splendid view of the outside parkland.

Like Diana's own childhood home in Norfolk, Highgrove is very much a family home, a place in which to bring up children. Upstairs, a galleried landing serves four main bedrooms, each with its own dressing-room. In addition to the nursery wing—which consists of a day nursery and two bedrooms —there are, higher still, a further five bedrooms. Down-stairs, in addition to the main rooms, are what house agents describe as 'the usual domestic offices'. There is a wine cellar and a boiler room for central heating. The grounds around the house include a kitchen garden with greenhouse and potting-sheds.

All her young life until now the Princess had been well accustomed to doing things for herself. As a bachelor girl, she had shared the chores of her London home with her three flatmates, doing her share of the cooking—she took a course in cookery after leaving school—and the washing up. She had always done her own shopping. Now, on the couple's first day at Highgrove, finding herself short of a nailbrush, she decided to slip into Tetbury and buy one. It was not the first time she had visited Tetbury. She had been there before marriage with Prince Charles on the same day that they had visited Cheltenham to meet police officers who would be responsible for their security once they had moved into Highgrove.

If Diana's spontaneous behaviour on their tour of Wales foreshadowed a new era in royal public life, a Princess of Wales prepared to pop out and do her own shopping suggested an equally new attitude to royal personal life. A few days later found her again shopping in Tetbury. This time it was a particular magazine she was seeking.

Even in Britain, few people outside Gloucestershire had heard of Tetbury, let alone Highgrove, until Charles and Diana moved in. Now, as the country home of the Prince and Princess of Wales, it was suddenly a household name to rank with Balmoral and Sandringham, a very desirable part of the country in which to live. A three-bedroomed cottage just across the road from Highgrove, empty for three years since the death of the previous owner, suddenly became one of the most sought-after properties in Britain. News that it was for sale resulted in hundreds of eager inquiries. Ordinarily, said the estate agent handling the sale, it would have sold for perhaps £20,000. Sensibly, he decided to auction it. The bidding actually started at £20,000 and went up to £37,000 before the property was knocked down to a middle-aged couple who insisted that they were more concerned with moving closer to their married daughter than with having the Prince and Princess of Wales as near neighbours.

That weekend Charles and Diana travelled from Highgrove to Broadlands, the Mountbatten home in Hampshire at which they had spent the first few nights of their honeymoon. This time their visit was to attend the christening in Romsey Abbey of

Nicholas Knatchbull, baby son of Lord Romsey and great-grandson of the murdered Earl Mountbatten. They returned to Highgrove by way of Blenheim Palace, where they enjoyed a recital by the English Chamber Orchestra. Charles also took advantage of the move into Highgrove to go hunting again, though not with the Beaufort with which he had sometimes hunted previously in the company of his sister and her husband. Aware that public feeling runs high on the subject of his fox-hunting forays—'Squalid behaviour', Lord Soper once derided it—he decided to join the less well known Vale of the White Horse Hunt for a day in the field. All in all, it proved to be a somewhat dispiriting outing. Largely unrecognized when he joined the hunt initially, he subsequently became separated from the other riders, was identified when he was obliged to dismount in order to open a gate and, with sightseers and reporters starting to follow him, eventually decided to call it a day.

A public announcement of his wife's pregnancy could not be delayed indefinitely. However, it was thought wiser to say nothing until after the following week's State Opening of Parliament, which Diana would be attending for the first time as Princess of Wales. The very fact that she was going at all, it was reasoned, would bring crowds in their thousands out onto the London streets. News that she was expecting a baby would have the effect of increasing the crowds perhaps tenfold, with all the additional policing and security problems that that would involve. It could end up being like the wedding day all over again.

So, except for family and a few close friends, people were still largely unaware that the Princess was pregnant when she and Charles attended the 25th London Film Festival at the National Film Theatre to see a showing of Peter Weir's much-praised Australian film, *Gallipoli*. For the occasion, the Princess wore a dress of bottle-green velvet with a Puritan-style collar in heavy white lace which, though romantic looking, was very different from the daringly strapless gown she had worn for her very first public appearance with Charles shortly before the wedding. Rather maternal-looking, some people thought the dress, not realizing how close they were to the truth.

And her pregnancy was still a secret, though a skiing holiday she and Charles had planned for the coming winter had been

quietly cancelled, when she again climbed into the Glass Coach
which a few months before had conveyed her to her wedding in
St Paul's. This time, in company with Prince Charles, his sister,
Princess Anne, and her husband, Mark Phillips, she was on her
way to Westminster, to the House of Lords, to the State Opening
of Parliament, the first Princess of Wales to attend that ancient
ceremony for nearly three-quarters of a century. For such a
traditional royal occasion she dressed in traditional royal
fashion, in a simple dress in white and silver, full skirted and
with a V-neck. She wore a pearl choker at her throat, and her
hair, bouffant-styled for the occasion, was topped by a tiara.
The State Opening of Parliament is a solemn occasion, far
removed from the happy-go-lucky walkabouts of the Welsh
tour, and such few smiles as she permitted herself while the
ancient ceremony ran its ponderous course were understandably
tentative and nervous.

She was still wearing the pearl choker that evening, though
she had changed into an off-the-shoulder dress, when she and
Charles went to the Victoria and Albert Museum for a preview
of the 'Splendours of Gonzaga' exhibition, the largest collection
of Renaissance art seen outside Italy for many years. Though
initially she seemed as lively as ever, pregnancy and the strain of
her earlier attendance at the State Opening of Parliament began
to tell on her as the evening wore on. It was perhaps concern for
her which caused Charles to muff his speech. 'On Sunday
evening we were at Blenheim . . . on Tuesday evening we went
to . . . what was it?' he asked, turning to Diana. She smiled and
shrugged. Then he remembered that it was the National Film
Theatre. 'It must be old age,' he quipped by way of excuse.

They stayed to watch an excerpt from Gagliano's opera *La
Dafne*, commissioned by the Gonzagas in the seventeenth
century, and were expected to go on to the Italian Embassy for
dinner with the President of the Italian Senate, Amintore
Fanfani. But Diana did not feel up to it and slipped quietly
away, leaving Charles to attend the Embassy dinner on his own.
His wife's absence clearly required an explanation, and thus it
was that the Italian Ambassador, Andrea Cagiati, became the
first person who was not a relative or close friend to learn of her
pregnancy. 'I am sorry the Princess is unable to come,' Prince
Charles told him, 'but she is expecting a child.'

Next day came the official announcement that the Princess

was pregnant, and the whole world shared the news. The wording of the announcement was yet another sign of changing times and changing attitudes. When the Queen was expecting her first baby, some thirty years earlier, the announcement was discretion itself. No mention, in fact, that she was actually going to have a baby at all. It said simply: 'Her Royal Highness The Princess Elizabeth, Duchess of Edinburgh, will undertake no public engagements after the end of June.' Of course, in those more modest days nearly everyone knew how to interpret that form of wording. By contrast, the 1981 announcement concerning the Princess of Wales not only made it crystal clear that she 'is expecting a baby' but said when—'in June next year'—and went on to mention her health—'excellent'—before adding that she 'hopes to continue to undertake some public engagements, but regrets any disappointment which may be caused by any curtailment of her planned programme'.

The announcement was made on 5 November, the day when the fact that Guy Fawkes and his fellows did not succeed in blowing up the Houses of Parliament is anomalously celebrated by lighting bonfires and discharging fireworks. In Tetbury and elsewhere, that night, the bonfires and fireworks did double duty by also celebrating the coming birth of an heir to the throne. The luncheon which Charles and Diana attended at London's Guildhall, though it had nothing to do with the birth of a baby when it was originally arranged, similarly became an occasion for special celebration. The two of them were in high spirits, talking and giggling together over a lunch of sole tarragon, filet of beef, orange soufflé and cheese. The Lord Mayor of London, Colonel Sir Ronald Gardner-Thorpe, decided to add a few congratulatory phrases to his prepared speech for the occasion. The couple's wedding, he said, had provided a memory 'that glows with the everlasting lustre of a gold ingot . . . an ingot that has now been supremely hallmarked by this morning's announcement that Your Royal Highnesses are to be blessed with a child, for which we all rejoice. Babies are bits of star-dust blown by the hand of God.'

If these rather fulsome phrases have all the appearance of something hastily tacked on, the Prince himself seemed to be completely unprepared to talk about babies, star-dust or anything of that nature. His speech concentrated on the wedding-day and the more recent tour of Wales, the success of which, he said, was 'entirely due to the effect my dear wife has on everybody'. It was not until after luncheon and speech-making were over that, responding to personal congratulations, he spoke of the baby. 'Naturally I am absolutely delighted. It is wonderful and of course I feel like any prospective father. My wife is overjoyed as well. A baby will be marvellous.'

As news of the royal announcement spread, shop assistants and secretaries, bank messengers and typists slipped out onto the streets in the hope of catching a glimpse of the mother-to-be as she and her husband left the Guildhall. Back at the palace, the first messages of congratulation and good wishes were already arriving. Gifts for the baby soon followed. Among the first was a pair of hand-knitted white bootees which four-year-old Helen Davies handed to the Queen when she journeyed north to open the Tyneside Metro the following day. 'That was quick work,' the Queen congratulated the child, though the bootees had in fact been knitted by Helen's aunt.

Would Diana have a boy or a girl? The answer is growing up now in the person of Prince William, but that was the question on everyone's lips at the time. A firm of bookmakers offered 125-to-one against the Princess having twins, which seemed very good odds in the circumstances. The birth of twins is by no means unknown in Diana's family tree. Her maternal grandfather inherited the Fermoy title only because he was born minutes ahead of his twin brother, and there are twins too among her cousins' families.

The problem of how to overcome the unknown boy or girl factor occupied the minds of souvenir-manufacturers, gleefully rubbing their hands at the prospect of another bonanza from commemorative mugs and jugs, plates and plaques, so soon after the royal wedding. Of more constitutional importance was the fact that the baby's sex might determine whether or not it succeeded to the throne in the fulness of time. As the firstborn son of the Prince of Wales, Prince William was to become second in line to the throne immediately he was born. But it might have been otherwise. Had William been Wilhelmina, then, as things stand, she would have been next in line after Charles only if her parents did not later have a son to displace her.

There was, inevitably, some small degree of disappointment in Australia, New Zealand and Canada that the pregnancy would mean postponing the planned visits to those countries by the Prince and Princess. The Queen may have toured Canada when she was pregnant with Prince Andrew, but that was at an earlier stage of pregnancy and, in the event, had proved to be a very considerable ordeal for her.

Amidst all the rejoicing at the announcement throughout Britain, the Commonwealth and elsewhere, there was only one discordant note. That long-time critic of the Royal Family William Hamilton MP was quoted as saying: 'It didn't take them long to get the production line rolling, did it?'

5 A Very Public Pregnancy

Being Princess of Wales, as Diana was soon to discover, offers no special dispensation when it comes to being pregnant, and she was to experience the same pangs of morning sickness and allied mother-to-be disorders and discomforts as any other young wife. 'No one told me it would be like this,' she sighed. Nor had anyone warned her that, *because* she was Princess of Wales, her pregnancy would mean an additional upset peculiar to her special position.

Early on in pregnancy, like many other young mother-to-be, more than anything else she wanted to rest and be quiet. To this end, she and Charles retreated to Highgrove, their country home, the longest spell they had enjoyed there together since moving in. From time to time they invited relatives and friends to visit them and see the house, among them Diana's sister Lady Sarah McCorquodale and one of Charles' close friends, Nicholas Soames, and his wife. But there were also other visitors to the area, if not to the house itself, who were uninvited and decidedly unwelcome. They were Press photographers hoping to obtain the sort of pictures of the Princess of Wales in pregnancy which editors would consider worth more than a thousand words.

They lay in wait outside the house, stalked the Princess on those rare occasions that she ventured out. From their own point of view, their patience was crowned with some degree of success. One managed to get a picture of Charles and Diana hugging each other as they emerged from the house with Diana's sister to see her off. Another danced backwards in front of the Princess, camera clicking, when she went shopping in Tetbury.

Until she emerged into the public spotlight as the future wife of a future king, Diana had been accustomed to the same freedom of action as any other young woman. She had been free to slip out to the shops when she felt like it, go to work, drive around in her car, sometimes cycle, visit her hairdresser, stop to chat to friends in the street. Even when her romance with Prince Charles first became public property and the newspapers homed in on her, she had not permitted the fact to change her way of life to any appreciable extent. She had stood up well to the unaccustomed pressure and continued to live her life much as usual.

It was inevitable, of course, as she realized, that much of her life would change with her metamorphosis into Princess of Wales, that to a large extent she would become public property, but she had still hoped for a degree of privacy in which she could be herself, enjoy some personal freedom and live as informally as she had done in bachelor-girl days. It might no longer be possible for her to go shopping in Harrods without photographers stalking her, but she had hoped it would be possible in somewhere as quiet and remote as Tetbury. Even this was denied her, it seemed. Subject as she was also to the emotional tension of pregnancy, the knowledge that photographers lay constantly in wait for her outside the house more and more unnerved her. She felt frightened to venture out; a prisoner in her own home.

She became increasingly upset, and her state of mind had its natural effect upon Prince Charles. An understanding and protective husband, he became 'hopping mad' at the pressure being heaped upon his young wife at a time when she was pregnant with their first child. The situation was discussed with his mother, the Queen. Brought up from birth to live with the restrictions placed upon the personal lives of those born royal, the Queen has long since become so accustomed to them that she perhaps is now scarcely aware of them. But she was quick to understand the effect those same restrictions could have on a daughter-in-law who had not previously been accustomed to them, and her sympathies were entirely with Diana.

In an attempt to relieve the pressure on the Princess and resolve an increasingly unhappy situation, a conference of national newspaper editors and television and radio chiefs was convened at Buckingham Palace. 'We expected that, following the honeymoon, Press attention would wane somewhat,' the Queen's Press officer, Michael Shea, told them. 'But it has in no way abated. The Princess of Wales feels totally beleaguered. She has coped extremely well; she has come through with flying colours. But now those who love her and care for her are getting anxious at the reaction it is having.'

He appealed for some let-up in the photographic pressure to which the Princess was subject, asking editors not to use photographs of her which had been obtained by invading her privacy. And, with the year 1981 approaching its end, he appealed in particular for her to be given 'some sort of a break' when she and her husband went to Sandringham with others of the Royal Family for the new year. There was, he said, no objection to the publication of photographs taken on public occasions, and almost as he said it photographers were busy pointing their cameras at Diana as she arrived, at the wheel of her own small car, on a visit to St Mary's Primary School in Tetbury to fulfil a promise made when she and Charles first moved into Highgrove. There had been pictures too the evening before, when she and her husband had gone together to the parish church to attend a concert in aid of the church restoration fund and the Benjamin Britten Foundation (which helps young musicians).

That the royal Press officer, in appealing to newspapers and television to give the Princess 'a break', was speaking very much on behalf of her mother-in-law was made abundantly plain by the Queen herself. Before the conference broke up, she took the unusual step of herself joining it to speak informally with those present, emphasizing and underlining what her Press officer had said.

'Totally beleaguered' though she felt herself to be at this early stage of pregnancy, the Princess, in one respect at least, was considerably more fortunate than her mother-in-law had been when she found herself pregnant with her third child, Prince Andrew. The planned visits that Charles and Diana were to have made to various Commonwealth countries—Australia, New Zealand and Canada—were sufficiently far into the future to be postponed without too much difficulty when Diana found herself pregnant. The Queen, some twenty-two years earlier, had been within a week or so of flying out to Canada when, after a gap of nearly ten years since the birth of Princess Anne, she found herself unexpectedly pregnant again. It was characteristically dutiful of her that she should have refused to have the tour postponed or even curtailed at such short notice, but insisted on going through with it in full (though there was one

The Prince and Princess of Wales on the steps of St Paul's Cathedral after
the wedding ceremony, 29 July 1981

Posing for the formal group photograph in the throne room of Buckingham
Palace, the bride and groom share a private joke

Diana's mother, the Hon. Mrs Frances Shand-Kydd, leaving St Paul's after the wedding

The Princess's father, Earl Spencer and Lady Spencer outside Buckingham Palace shortly after the engagement was announced

The Prince of Wales steals a kiss from his bride. On the balcony with the newlyweds are *(left to right)* Prince Philip, the Queen Mother, the two pages Nicholas Windsor and Edward Van Cutsem, three of the bridesmaids Sarah-Jane Gaselee, Catherine Cameron and Clementine Hambro, and the Queen

Charles and Diana drive to Waterloo Station on their way to Broadlands and the start of their honeymoon

Honeymoon couple aboard the royal yacht *Britannia* off Gibraltar

Brian Organ's informal
portraits of Charles and
Diana, unveiled at the
National Portrait Gallery
on 13 February and
23 July 1981
respectively.

Their first tour: the royal couple with Lord Snowdon, Constable of Caernarvon Castle, at the start of a tour of the Welsh principality, October 1981

Diana meets the Cubs, and accepts a kiss at Builth Wells

The Gloucestershire home of Charles and Diana: Highgrove, near Tetbury

Prince Charles leaves home

Unnoticed by neighbours, Diana goes shopping in Tetbury

Visiting the Guildhall for lunch with the Lord Mayor of London, the day Diana's pregnancy was announced

An expectant Princess at ITN's London studios with
newscaster Carol Barnes *(right)*, who was also expecting
a baby at the time, and Selina Scott

Showered with gifts and good wishes for the baby at Chesterfield

day when she was forced to remain in bed instead of going to Dawson City). As a result, parts of the tour became a considerable ordeal for her, with the situation hardly helped by the decision that her pregnancy must remain secret until the tour was over and she was back home. In the event, total secrecy proved impossible, and journalists accompanying the royal party were not entirely deceived by the 'upset tummy' and other excuses trotted out to account for those occasions when the Queen was so obviously indisposed.

There was no need for such lame excuses as 'upset tummy' to be used on behalf of the Princess of Wales. With the whole world fully aware that she was pregnant, people were understanding and sympathetic, if disappointed, when Charles was obliged to turn up alone at public functions which they had arranged to attend together. Plagued by morning sickness, she was unable to go with him to the Chippenham fat-stock show, for instance, to Falmouth, where he opened the new Maritime Rescue Co-ordination Centre (and was given a miniature toothbrush for the expected baby) or to various Duchy of Cornwall properties they had earlier planned to visit together. But she was with him and other members of the Royal Family at the Albert Hall for the annual British Legion Festival of Remembrance. Dressed appropriately in black with a touch of lace at the throat and wrists, she also joined the two oldest of her in-laws, the Queen Mother and Princess Alice of Gloucester, on a balcony in Whitehall to watch her husband and his parents place Remembrance Day wreaths on the Cenotaph. But she was not well enough to join him for a similar wreath-laying ceremony on Horse Guards Parade that afternoon nor on a planned visit to the Welsh Guards, of which Prince Charles is Colonel. Nor could she travel with him to the West Country the following day for the annual Duchy of Cornwall dinner in Devon.

'She is quite all right,' Charles was quick to reassure those he met at the dinner, 'but it is better for her not to do too many things at present. You've all got wives—you know the problem.'

Tenant farmers at that Duchy of Cornwall function may have understood the problem he referred to, but certainly none of their wives had ever been pregnant with a baby who would be second in line to the throne. Diana was, and this created another special problem quite apart from the trouble she had been

having with Press photographers. This was the question of where
the baby should be born.

There is no particular tradition that the heir to the throne
should be born at Buckingham Palace. It is true that Prince
Charles himself was born at the palace, in an outsize bathroom
which had been converted into a delivery ward for the occasion,
but only because his grandfather, King George VI, wanted his
first grandchild born under his own roof. The Queen was
similarly born at her grandparents' London home, but they
were her maternal grandparents and the home in question was
in Bruton Street. It can be argued, of course, that at the time the
Queen was born there was no expectation that she would one
day succeed to the throne. The same argument can be applied to
her father, who was born at Sandringham where his parents
were living at the time. But his eldest brother, who was born heir
to the throne—and did indeed reign briefly as King Edward
VIII before abdicating to marry Mrs Simpson—came into the
world at White Lodge, Richmond, the home of his maternal
grandparents. His father, King George V, was born at
Marlborough House in London, while George V's elder
brother, who would have succeeded to the throne had he lived,
was born at Frogmore in Windsor Great Park.

Princess Anne was born at Clarence House where the Queen
(then still Princess Elizabeth) and Prince Philip were living at
the time. Andrew and Edward, like Charles, were born at
Buckingham Palace. But by then the Princess had become
Queen Elizabeth II; the palace was now her home, and it was
the custom of the time for babies to be born at home. Attitudes to
childbirth have changed since then. These days it is considered
wiser and safer for young mothers, and especially first-time
mothers, to have their babies in the more hygienic surroundings
of a hospital where everything is immediately at hand in the
event of an unexpected emergency. St Mary's Hospital in
Paddington has become a favourite choice of the Royal
Family—Princess Anne had both her babies there—and Diana,
visiting a friend who had just had a baby in St Mary's, took the
opportunity to check on the accommodation and facilities
available in the private wing of the hospital.

The on-and-off indispositions of early pregnancy were still
troubling Diana when she accompanied her husband on a visit
to York and Chesterfield. She looked pale and tired as they

walked together round the National Railway Museum in York and rode on a replica of Stephenson's *Rocket*. Her husband, however, was in fine spirits. Collecting 'old loos' was a hobby of his, he told staff at the Railway Museum. 'If you are ever getting rid of any, I'd like to buy one.' Then it was on by helicopter to Chesterfield, where they opened a new shopping precinct and a new police headquarters as well as attending a thanksgiving service in the parish church with its crooked spire.

If she seemed slightly more subdued than she had been in Wales, Diana was still the girl 'who tried hardest' as she small-talked her way through crowds so thick they brought traffic to a standstill. It was only natural that people in the crowd should ask her if she wanted a boy or a girl. 'I don't mind as long as it's healthy,' she replied. There was a lighthearted exchange with someone else about tooth fairies, which, with the baby not yet born, seemed to be looking rather far ahead. As in Wales, those accompanying the Princess almost vanished under the piles of flowers thrust upon her. In Wales people had not yet known that she was expecting a baby. In York and Chesterfield they did, and flowers were accompanied by gifts for the baby, cuddly toys, ducks for the bath, and a whole nursery wardrobe of bootees, mittens and baby clothes quickly and hurriedly knitted by pensioners and schoolgirls alike. By the time the walkabout in Chesterfield was over, two accompanying police cars were crammed to capacity. In all this fuss over the Princess and the baby she was expecting, the baby's father was not entirely overlooked. A group of Morris dancers brought along a fertility symbol for him. It was 'a bit late for that', he said.

Charles' birthday, 14 November, that year fell on a Saturday. To make sure of celebrating it quietly and privately, they travelled alone together to Sandringham, the first time they had been there since before their marriage. But the people of the district saw little or nothing of them. They kept very much to themselves, staying not at the 'big house', with its dozens of rooms, but three miles away in a brick and sandstone farmhouse on the fringe of the marshes at Wolferton. Small by royal standards, cosy, isolated, tucked away at the end of a road leading nowhere, with woods and fields on one side, the marshes and the sea on the other, Wood Farm had stood empty and unused for several years when the Queen renovated and converted it initially to serve as a weekend retreat for Charles during his time at Cambridge University. On the occasion that the Queen herself first stayed there with her family it was still so cramped that Andrew and Edward had to share a bedroom. Since then an old barn has been converted to provide two further bedrooms. Even so, it is still inclined to bulge at the seams when the whole family is there.

Diana and Charles, that weekend of his thirty-third birthday, had the place to themselves, their peace and solitude broken only by the clucking of chickens and the mooing of cattle. The wife of a local farmworker came in to cook their meals, and of an evening they watched television together. To the disappointment of the locals, Sunday did not find them putting in an appearance at the parish church. Instead, they went for a walk across the fields, dog at heel and Charles with gun in hand in the hope of getting a pot-shot at something.

On their way back to Highgrove they stopped off near Newmarket to visit Prince Charles' friend Hugh van Cutsem, whose small son had been one of the pages at their wedding. But Diana's respite from the upsets of pregnancy was short-lived. A further bout of morning sickness, later in the week, prevented her from accompanying Charles on another planned visit to the West Country. Nor was she able to go with him to Horfield, where he went round the Remploy factory in addition to visiting a community centre and a school. The schoolchildren were particularly disappointed that he did not have Diana with him. The factory visit found him in jocular vein. Shown the medical corsets made there, he quipped, 'I have a nasty feeling I shall need one before long. My wife keeps trying to feed me up.'

However, Diana was well enough to fulfil the engagement listed in her appointments diary as her first solo venture, the switching on of the Christmas illuminations in London's West End. 'I'm fine; feeling much better,' she said brightly to those who inquired. And not only feeling better, but courageous with it. Though it was little more than a week since a bomb-disposal expert had been killed while trying to defuse an IRA bomb planted in adjoining Oxford Street, she stood in full view of everyone on a balcony in Regent Street to perform the ceremony, an attractive figure in a suit of blue velvet trimmed with silver piping. Prince Charles, watching on television at home, was perhaps more nervous for her than she was for herself.

While police continued to search lock-up garages throughout

London for a store of gelignite the IRA was believed to have hidden away, the Princess was out and about in the capital again the next day, this time in the company of her husband. Together they planted a number of flowering cherry trees in the vicinity of the Royal Thames Yacht Club. Diana planted one to commemorate the coming birth of the baby, giggling a little as Charles encircled her with his arms in order to help her with the spade, and two more to commemorate their wedding. Charles on his own planted three more trees to the memory of his murdered great-uncle, Earl Mountbatten.

Another solo engagement, at Northampton this time, gave the Princess a chance to drop in on her father at Althorp. The Northampton engagement, the opening of a new post office, also afforded her a convenient opportunity to send her royal in-laws a congratulatory telegram on the occasion of their thirty-fourth wedding anniversary. Unable to stay long with her father on that occasion, she returned privately to Althorp later in the week to spend more time with him. While there, she also seized the chance of slipping into Northampton on a shopping excursion, patiently waiting her turn to pay for some cards and newspapers before crossing the street to a chemist's shop.

She did not attend the annual reception for members of the Diplomatic Corps which the Queen gave at Buckingham Palace, though Prince Charles did. But she was with him, though looking perhaps a little out of her depth for once, at a palace luncheon for members of the European Council. With the Queen and Prince Philip, the couple handed over special cars to a number of disabled people under the Motability Scheme. In contrast to her seeming shyness at the European Council luncheon, Diana looked vibrant and radiant, romantic too in a silver-sequined gown and velvet cloak, when she and Charles attended a special performance of the ballet *Romeo and Juliet* at the Royal Opera House. It was very much a family occasion. Also in the party were Diana's two sisters, Sarah and Jane, together with their husbands, Charles' brother, Prince Andrew, and Princess Margaret's son, Viscount Linley. Music-lovers as they are, Charles and Diana were again at the Royal Opera House only five nights later, this time to hear the Spanish tenor Placido Domingo sing *Tosca*.

In the weeks leading up to Christmas, Diana drove several times in secret to Buckingham Palace. Once there, safe from prying eyes, she again donned her elaborate wedding-dress with its headdress and veil to pose for a portrait being painted by Sue Ryder. Most royal portraits, like the one by Bryan Organ for which she had sat earlier, are commissioned to adorn national art galleries, government buildings, armed forces' establishments and the like. But this one was different. It had been commissioned personally by Prince Charles as a memento of their wedding day. The finished portrait, seen briefly by those of the public who visited the annual exhibition of the Royal Society of Portrait Painters a few months later, was in very different mood from that earlier portrait by Bryan Organ, less contemporary in both pose and execution, far more romantic. The art critic of the *Tatler* did not like it at all. 'I've never seen anything so awful,' he opined. Others were of different opinion. Artist June Mendoza thought it 'a charming picture'. For many people, it depicted the Princess as they like to think of her, a porcelain figurine, demure, vulnerable and romantic. And that is surely how Prince Charles himself sees her, and the image of her he wishes to be remembered in the years ahead.

That the Princess is a romantic at heart showed in a small incident around the time the 'wedding-day' portrait was being painted. She and Charles were attending a carol concert arranged in aid of the Prince's Trust. While there, they listened sympathetically while unemployed teenagers spoke of the depression they felt at their inability to find work, and one young trainee silversmith, Nigel Corham, showed them a silver pendant he had made. It was a gift for his girl-friend, he said. Diana smiled tenderly. 'Everyone loves a love story,' she told him.

In the approach to Christmas they drove through the snow to Guildford Cathedral for an interdenominational service at which Prince Charles read the lesson. He also took the opportunity to express something of his feeling concerning events in Poland. 'This Christmas we should think particularly about the Poles,' he said. 'Throughout their long history they seem to have suffered so much. Perhaps one day their faith, courage and warm humanity deserves to be rewarded.' After the service, braving the elements, the two of them joined the crowd gathered outside the cathedral in singing 'We Wish You A Merry Christmas'. And for Charles and Diana, a very merry Christmas it proved to be, at Windsor with other members of the

Royal Family, with gifts being exchanged on Christmas Eve in the royal tradition under a tree ablaze with lights, a dinner of Norfolk turkey and all the trimmings followed by brandy-flamed plum pudding, and, in the evening, a sing-song and the fun of playing charades, a game which has been a royal favourite since Queen Alexandra's day at least.

From Windsor, with the Queen and Prince Philip, they went to Sandringham for the New Year, though Diana did not enjoy the stay there as much as Charles did. He was in his element bagging pheasants, as kings and princes have done at Sandringham since his great-great-grandfather first acquired the estate nearly a century and a quarter before. Diana was somewhat less happy at being expected to accompany him on his shooting sorties. For all her country upbringing, she does not like blood sports, her relatives say.

More worrying than any small marital tiff they may have had on the subject of pheasant shooting was a fall Diana had one day while descending the stairs. For her, in this respect, Sandringham would seem to be an unlucky place. The local newspaper for 1963, when she was two, reports her as having fallen down some stone steps. At the age of nine there was a fall from her pony which resulted in a broken arm and has left her nervous of riding to this day. In 1982, at the age of twenty, a slight stumble as she came downstairs saw her fall the remainder of the flight. She was helped back to bed, and Charles stayed with her until a doctor arrived to examine her. Happily, both mother-to-be and the baby she was expecting proved to be uninjured, and, after resting in bed for a time, she was able to get up again and go out.

It was while the family was at Sandringham that the Queen gave her formal approval to a new coat-of-arms to be shared by her son and his bride. The new arms, featured now on the flag flying over their country home and the smaller ones which adorn their cars, have the shield of the Prince of Wales leaning against that of the House of Spencer with lion and unicorn supporters. Below the shields are the feathers of the Prince of Wales and his motto, '*Ich Dien*' ('I serve').

Diana had always felt that her family had received rather scant treatment in the allocation of seats in St Paul's Cathedral at the time of the wedding. To compensate, shortly after Christmas, she and her husband journeyed to her father's stately

home in Northamptonshire in order to entertain people from
the family estate who had not received wedding invitations.
With Althorp closed to the public for the weekend, the royal
couple spent some three hours mingling with and talking to
tenant farmers and their wives, estate workers and theirs,
household servants and those who act as guides when the house
is open to the public. They found Diana's father somewhat
saddened by the thought that he would almost certainly have to
sell more of the family's art treasures—a number of paintings,
including a Reynolds shipped to America, had already been
sold—if the house itself, which has been in the family since the
sixteenth century, was to be maintained in a suitable state of
repair. It was only sensible though, he felt, to sell some of the art
treasures in order to establish a fund to preserve those that
remained, along with Althorp itself.

A few days later there was an outing of a very different kind
when the couple, with Diana's pregnancy now physically
visible, went along to the Dick Shepherd Comprehensive School
in Tulse Hill. Arriving there, they found a 'school fair' in
progress, with the necessity for them to buy tickets at the various
stalls. There was immediately a snag: Royalty never carries
money (except for church-going on Sundays). However,
temporary small loans from their accompanying detectives
enabled them to pay their way. They each had an unsuccessful
go at guessing the weight of a homemade cake and also invested
in some tombola tickets. Charles paid 50p. for six tickets and
won nothing. Diana, more cautiously, spent 25p. on three
tickets and found that she had won a set of plastic picnic cutlery.
However, they were not required to pay for everything and left
again heaped with gifts galore, among them an outsize loaf
made from a traditional Jamaican recipe and baked in the shape
of a duck, a badge inscribed 'Charlie Is My Darling', a toy corgi
and yet more clothes for the expected baby.

In time off from royal duties, Charles continued to ride to
hounds. He was out hunting the day Diana journeyed to Eaton
Hall, the home of the Duke and Duchess of Westminster, to
stand as godmother to their second child, Edwina. By now more
than 150 requests had been received for the Princess to become
patron or president of various organizations. Her interest in
children showed in those she decided to accept initially, among
them the Pre-School Play-Groups Association, Albany (a

Deptford community centre dealing with children at risk) and the Malcolm Sargent Cancer Fund for Children. Others she picked were the Royal School for the Blind and the Welsh National Opera. It is a small start which will assuredly grow considerably in the future, though it is doubtful if she will ever catch up with the enormous number of organizations with which her husband is connected. Everyone around her agreed that she had settled quickly and successfully into her new role as a professional princess. Public engagements intended as 'try-outs' had turned into triumphs. Even so, the presence of Press and television cameras still seemed to have a slightly inhibiting effect at times. It might help, it was felt, if Diana knew something of what went on behind the scenes. To this end, it was arranged for her to visit the studios of International Television News where she watched a typical news programme being compiled and transmitted.

Prince Charles is perhaps better known for his witty, off-the-cuff remarks than for his serious speeches, but he can speak seriously enough when the subject is a serious one, as he did to the London Press Club in February 1982. His theme on that occasion was 'Freedom'. Following upon the remarks he had made about Poland during that pre-Christmas visit to Guildford Cathedral, it was clearly something much on his mind and to which he had given a good deal of thought. After pointing out that only one-third of the world's population live in countries which practise democracy as a Western European or American understands it, he went on:

'The most insidious enemies of liberty are those who tell us that they know us and our true needs better than we do ourselves. For they are wise and we are foolish or blind or misled. One day we shall ourselves grow up—as a result of obeying their orders—and we shall then realize how right they were to coerce us in our own interest.

'If we mind about what we call our freedom, what exactly are we trying to preserve? Surely it is our integrity as individuals; our right not to be treated as a collective mass which can be manipulated as so much malleable human material.

'Presumably we wish to avoid becoming like bricks in a building to be constructed by the infallible architect—bricks which, if they do not fit, must be eliminated or "re-educated". The Gulag archipelago.'

His speech contained a particular message for the journalists listening to him: 'Every tyrant, whether of the Left or Right, always begins by curtailing or suppressing the Freedom of the Press, so that writers must dance to tunes called by the organs of the party or army or Government.'

The meaning of freedom becomes clear, the Prince continued, only when it is taken away . The problem, as he saw it, was to learn from the experiences of those who had lost their liberty so that we could take steps to protect our own. For Charles, it was a long, thoughtful—and thought-provoking —speech which ended: 'Our protection depends, I believe, on the mystical power which from time immemorial has been called God and whose relationship to man seems to depend on man's relationship to his inner voice.' He added this tailpiece: 'It also depends, dare I say it, on a free Press which is constantly aware of its vital, responsible and extraordinarily powerful voice.'

If that final remark was also intended as a hint to the newspapers, it was one which fell on deaf ears in some editorial offices. And the thanks which Prince Charles extended to Fleet Street during the course of his visit to the Press Club for the breathing space which he and, more especially, Diana had been afforded proved to be a shade premature. The holiday with Fleet Street was over, even if the royal couple were themselves off on holiday.

It was mid-February, with Diana slightly more than halfway through her term of pregnancy and Britain gripped in a spell of bitterly cold weather, when she and Charles took off for the Bahamas on a ten-day vacation. With them went the Prince's Mountbatten relatives, Lord and Lady Romsey, whose holiday home they would be sharing on the pint-sized island of Eleuthera. Their seats on a scheduled British Airways flight had been booked, at a cost of £1,388 each for the round trip, in the name of Hardy. However, there was not the remotest possibility of 'Mrs Hardy' being mistaken for anyone but the Princess of Wales as, delighted at the prospect of an away-from-it-all holiday in the sun, she almost skipped up the aircraft steps. Her joy, unfortunately, was to be short-lived. Despite the Queen's earlier appeal for her daughter-in-law to be permitted more personal privacy during her spell of pregnancy, the temptation of obtaining photographs of the couple on holiday was to prove irresistible to some newspapers. Within hours of Charles and Diana flying out, photographers from Britain, Europe and America were already airborne in pursuit. Some of the American newspaper teams made the mistake (from their own point of view) of politely asking if they could photograph and interview the Prince and Princess. They were promptly ordered off the island. Others set about obtaining photographs, if not interviews, by stealth, while the really clever ones, tipped off in advance about the royal holiday plans, were already surveying the island for suitable photographic vantage-points before Charles and Diana had even arrived.

The following day found the couple enjoying themselves on the beach. Diana, despite her now obvious pregnancy, wore only a brief bikini. Together they paddled in the sea and sunbathed on the sand, with Diana cheerfully applying sun-tan oil to her husband's reddening back—both of them blissfully unaware that some two hundred yards away, in the thick undergrowth on the other side of the causeway, photographers were busy focusing their lenses and clicking their shutters. The photographers had, in fact, risen around four o'clock that morning to establish themselves in their 'hides' overlooking the beach before anyone else was about. Mission accomplished, they withdrew as cautiously as they had come.

Following on all that had gone before, the harassment of Diana in courtship days and the more recent incidents at Highgrove, the publication of those photographs in two of Britain's national tabloids, *The Sun* and the *Daily Star*, resulted in a storm of protest from palace and public alike. The Queen was as angry as she has ever been in her life and personally instructed Michael Shea, her chief Press officer, to make her displeasure abundantly clear to the newspapers concerned. What they had done, she said, angered her not as the Queen, not because of any invasion of royal privacy, but as a mother-in-law concerned for the health of her daughter-in-law and the well-being of the baby she was carrying. Making it very clear that he was speaking directly on behalf of the Queen, Shea told the newspapers bluntly, 'Such tasteless behaviour is a breach of normally accepted British Press standards in respect of the privacy of individuals. We have had many, many calls from the public saying how shocked and disgusted they are by the pictures, and we have also had support from other editors.'

In the House of Commons, Sir John Langford-Holt, Conservative Member of Parliament for Shrewsbury, tabled a motion regretting that the editors of the two tabloids 'should have fallen so short of the professional standards of journalism', while Kenneth Morgan, director of the Press Council, went on record as saying, 'Princesses as well as paupers are entitled to privacy unless some serious and legitimate public interest for intruding on their privacy can be found.' Both tabloids promptly recalled their reporters and photographers, while on Eleuthera, as soon as the reaction in Britain was known, other journalistic teams were rounded up and escorted to the local airport.

Both tabloids published editorials saying they were sorry, though both apologies were qualified. In one the editorial stated: 'The *Daily Star* has a special affection for Princess Diana. That is why we send her a message today: "If we have upset you, we are deeply sorry". Our interest was out of deep affection for the Royal couple. We were so pleased to see Diana enjoying herself so freely on the beach that we thought our readers would want to share her joy.' Newspapers around the world, the editorial continued, were eager to buy the pictures, some offering thousands of pounds. However, the editor had ordered that they should not be sold. 'Our only aim in photographing the Royal couple in a happy holiday mood was because we felt that the British public would want to know that Diana was looking so well and happy.'

The newspaper's Australian-born editor, Lloyd Turner, went on radio to add: 'I happen to believe that pregnancy is one of the most beautiful things that anybody can see.'

The *Daily Star*'s rival in royal displeasure said in its editorial: 'The pictures were carefree, innocent and delightful. They brought a breath of summer into the lives of millions of our readers back in chilly Britain. *The Sun* is concerned to hear that the pictures have upset the Royal couple. . . . Of course, it was never our intention to offend. If we have done so, we are deeply sorry. In all honesty, we see nothing wrong in pictures that could have been any young happy couple on a public beach.'

To prove how 'innocent and delightful' the photographs were, *The Sun* printed some of them all over again. Commented

Buckingham Palace: 'Just what one would expect from *The Sun*. It speaks for the attitude of the paper to the entire business. The readership of *The Sun* will come to their own conclusions. Most people find these pictures in the worst possible taste.' And the Press Council, when it later adjudicated on the matter, decided that *The Sun*'s apology was 'worthless' when it had not only re-printed some of the pictures along with its 'apology' but also re-sold them to foreign publications. Of the manner in which the photographs had been obtained, the Press Council had this to say: 'The surreptitious taking and publishing of these long-range pictures of the Princess of Wales on a beach when she was five months pregnant and wearing a bikini was a gross intrusion into her personal privacy. Whether the beach was public or private is immaterial. There was not legitimate public interest to excuse that intrusion. "In the public interest" is not synonymous with "of interest to the public". Personal consent would have been required for the publication of pictures in these circumstances by any woman who was pregnant.'

The first of the points made by the Press Council in its judgement would seem to be the important one. Whether those published pictures of the Prince and Princess on holiday were 'innocent and delightful', as *The Sun* maintained at the time, or 'in the worst possible taste', as Buckingham Palace insisted, was surely a secondary consideration to the peeping-Tom cir-cumstances in which the pictures were taken. The knowledge that she and her husband had been watched by hidden eyes when they thought themselves alone could have a profound psychological effect on any woman, let alone one in the mid-term stage of pregnancy and as shy and modest as the Princess. In other respects, however, the holiday benefited her. She returned to Britain looking sun-tanned and extremely fit physically, as Prince Charles did also. For her, the old royal rule of 'no further public engagements' in pregnancy did not apply, and she continued to fulfil her public commitments.

On a rainy March day she accompanied her husband to Westminster Abbey for a service to mark the centenary of the Royal College of Music. With them on that occasion, looking as indefatigable as ever in her eighty-second year, was the Queen Mother, who had played such an important part in their courtship. The Princess also accompanied her husband to the new Barbican Centre, opened by the Queen only the previous

day, on the occasion of a gala performance in aid of his Prince's
Trust as well as attending a charity preview of the play *The Little
Foxes*. Both functions were to see some lighthearted joking at
royal expense. At the Barbican, impersonator Mike Yarwood,
giving an impression of Prince Charles, gagged that the Princess
had entered a 'Diana look-alike' contest and ended up with
third prize. At the theatre, the cast stood in line for the
customary presentations to the royal guest of honour. As the
presentations ended and the Princess turned away, Elizabeth
Taylor, the star of the show, also began walking along the line in
mock regal fashion. However, Diana chanced to look back and
catch her in the act. Far from being offended, the Princess burst
out laughing.

Despite her elevation to royal status, Diana is not the sort of
girl to forget old friends, and an invitation from a school chum
found her journeying to Hampshire to see another Diana
—Diana Macdonald—marry a grandson of the Earl of
Lindsay. She enjoyed herself immensely in the company of
friends, happily talking over old times. She enjoyed herself
rather less the day she and Charles went to Cheltenham for the
running of the Gold Cup. Perhaps the cold weather had
something to do with her seeming lack of enthusiasm on that
occasion. Or perhaps, like many another mother-to-be, she
was beginning to find pregnancy a tediously drawn-out
affair.

If Diana was no different from many another expectant wife in
this respect, Charles, at times, could be as infuriating as any
other expectant father, full of good advice, confident that he
knew all about the problems of pregnancy. Anything he did not
know, he would look up in books on the subject. Prince Charles
is by no means the one hundred per cent macho male his
enthusiasm for hunting, shooting and polo-playing might
suggest. There is also a gentler, more artistic side to his
personality. If he no longer plays the cello, as he did in his
university days, he still finds time to paint upon occasion, and
around this time two of his water-colours, one of Suez which
they had visited during their honeymoon cruise, went on show
at an exhibition organized by the Royal Institute of Painters.
Collectors of royal memorabilia, however, were disappointed to
learn that they were not for sale.

But it was the fast-approaching birth of the baby which

largely pre-occupied husband and wife at this time. While Charles perused books on childbirth, Diana went shopping for baby-clothes. They had already been sent more than sufficient clothes to outfit a whole maternity ward of babies, mittens and bootees—'thousands of pairs', Charles said—vests and cardigans, many of them hand-knitted by loyal and industrious fingers, but it was surely no more than natural that the mother-to-be should prefer to make her own selection. The store she patronized declined to tell newspaper reporters what she had bought. 'We do not wish to appear to be using the Royal Family for advertisement,' said one of its directors. Others were sometimes less circumspect. The owners of a nursery boutique presented the royal parents-to-be with items of nursery furniture, among them a cot designed as a miniature four-poster. Then the story of this gift somehow found its way into the newspapers. Charles' private secretary promptly telephoned the boutique owners to convey royal displeasure. 'Gifts are accepted only on the understanding that there is no publicity,' Buckingham Palace explained. In the event, the baby's nursery was later furnished with items which, like his clothes, Diana had picked herself.

The upset over nursery furniture was not the only furore over gifts to the couple to erupt around this time. Two firms, one British, the other German, both of which had given them kitchen equipment at the time of their marriage, argued heatedly through the newspapers as to whose equipment had gone where. The British outfit insisted that their equipment had gone into the main kitchen at Highgrove while the German equipment had been relegated to one of the cottages on the estate. Not so, said the Germans; it was their equipment which had gone into the main house. As it happened, the Germans were wrong.

The whole question of gifts to members of the Royal Family on such special occasions as a birth or a wedding is a delicate and controversial one. So, indeed, is the question of royal visits to commercial enterprises. Gifts and visits alike are sometimes, even if inadvertently, subject to publicity, as when Diana, opening a new factory in Wales, was photographed wearing a hat with the name Sony on it. The difficulty is, of course, in knowing where the line should be drawn.

The question of whether the expected baby would prove to be

a boy or a girl continued to excite public interest. Though Diana
had said publicly that she didn't mind which it was—'Just as
long as it's healthy'—she and Charles were privately hoping
that it would turn out to be a boy. Certainly a firstborn son
would avoid any later change in the order of succession to the
throne. Only death could prevent his becoming Britain's king at
some future date. But a girl-child would not necessarily become
queen. She could be displaced at any time by a younger brother
born later. Some Members of Parliament sought to change this,
and a new Succession to the Crown Bill, endorsed by some
politicians of all four main parties and intended to give a girl
equal rights to those of a boy, was brought forward in
the House of Commons by Michael English, Labour Member of
Parliament for Nottingham West. Lacking official Government
support, however, it stood no chance of reaching the Statute
Book and, as things turned out, was to prove unnecessary, at
least in this generation.

Boy or girl, the baby would clearly need a nanny. Eager
though Diana was to bring up her baby herself as far as possible,
she was also alive to the fact that her duties as Princess of Wales
would necessarily continue, baby or no baby. Her own
upbringing, in any event, was geared to the idea that babies
have nannies; she had had one herself in her nursery days.
Unlike her sister-in-law, Princess Anne, who had fallen back on
the services of Nanny Anderson, who had looked after her in
childhood, Diana's feeling was for someone younger, a nanny
nearer her own age. It was through the family grapevine that she
came to hear of Barbara Barnes, nanny to the children of
Princess Margaret's friends, the Hon. Colin Tennant and his
wife, Anne. She had been with them for fourteen years, and the
Tennant children, a boy of fourteen and twin girls of eleven,
were now of an age when they no longer required a nanny. She
seemed to the Princess exactly the sort of person she was seeking:
firm yet kind, not at all starchy. There was also the small
personal link that she came from Diana's home county of
Norfolk. The Tennant parents recommended her strongly and
their children even more so—'smashing; a super nanny'. The
Princess decided to talk to Nanny Barnes for herself. The
answers she received to her questions—'I do not see any special
problems in bringing up a royal baby'. . . 'I treat all children as
individuals' . . . 'I believe in a mother being strongly involved in

bringing up her baby'—were very much in accordance with her own views, and Barbara Barnes got the job.

The Prince and Princess were still undecided as to whether or not the baby should be born in hospital. They talked things over with George Pinker, the royal gynaecologist. His advice supported their own feelings that a hospital birth was perhaps preferable, and a private room was booked at St Mary's, where Princess Anne had had her two babies. Provided they were at Kensington Palace when the Princess went into labour, it would involve only a short drive.

However, there was to be a deal more travelling before that. Despite Diana's now advanced state of pregnancy, they visited a number of provincial cities together, Newcastle upon Tyne, Leeds, Liverpool. So enthusiastic were the crowds during the royal walkabout at Newcastle upon Tyne that a ten-year-old boy was forced to the ground by the surge of people behind him, and his leg became trapped between two of the crush-barriers. Diana saw it happen, and she and Charles went to the boy's rescue. 'Please stop pushing,' Charles instructed those behind. The boy was extricated from between the crush-barriers, and the Princess helped him to his feet. 'Are you all right?' she asked him. He felt frightened, he told her. 'Don't worry,' she consoled him.

The expected baby was naturally a constant subject of small-talk during walkabouts. In Leeds, visiting St Gemma's Hospice, Diana was told by an old-age pensioner that he shared a birthdate with Prince Philip (10 June) and was hoping that the new royal baby would be born on the same day. 'It won't be,' Diana said, laughing. 'It's due on my birthday—1 July.' The baby, as time was to show, had other ideas.

The Princess's natural demonstrativeness was never more apparent than when she and Charles, on their visit to Liverpool, opened a new pagoda designed to serve as a cultural centre for the thousands of Chinese who live in the city. As she stepped from her car on arrival at the pagoda, a diminutive three-year-old dodged past the police cordon with a bunch of yellow tulips for her. Then, as Diana bent to take them from him, he flung his arms round her neck. 'I love you,' he murmured. Diana's warm-hearted nature could not fail to respond. Her arms went round the child and she kissed him.

That day in Liverpool was also the day Argentina invaded the

Falkland Islands. In the weeks which followed, with Charles'
brother Andrew flying a helicopter from the deck of HMS
Invincible, the royal couple shared the fear and concern of
thousands of others with relatives serving in the British Task
Force which was to regain the islands. For Charles, there was
also perhaps a measure of frustration at not being part of the
Task Force. All his adult life, because he thinks it important 'to
lead from the front', he has pushed himself, tested himself. 'In
some ways I envy my brother,' he confessed later, 'being able to
go and do what he did in the South Atlantic.' But if Charles
envied Andrew this opportunity to test himself to the ultimate,
Diana, now in the last three months of pregnancy, was doubtless
glad to have her husband safe at her side.

Lacking the real test of being part of what was going on in the
South Atlantic, Charles was forced to content himself with
making another dive in the Solent to see how the work of
salvaging the *Mary Rose*, King Henry VIII's ill-fated flagship,
was coming along. 'It really is in marvellous condition,' he said
enthusiastically when he surfaced again. A keen supporter of the
project from its inception, it was the ninth time he had dived
down to the wreck—and the last. Later that year the *Mary Rose*
was to be successfully brought to the surface from the watery
grave in which she had rested for all those centuries.

Because of her advanced state of pregnancy, the Princess took
no part in the public side of things during President and Mrs
Reagan's state visit to Britain that summer. She was not with her
husband and mother-in-law to greet the American President and
his wife when they arrived at Windsor Castle, shepherded by
Prince Philip; nor did she attend the state banquet given in their
honour. But she met them just the same, sitting and chatting
with them at a private dinner party on the first night of their
visit.

There were no lurking photographers to spoil things when she
and Charles enjoyed a brief four-day break in the Scilly Isles
that May. Back from that holiday, she insisted upon continuing
with a light spatter of public engagements until a very few weeks
before the baby was born.

The birth of the baby, as things turned out, was less than five
weeks away when she opened a Deptford community centre run
by Albany, one of the organizations of which she had recently
become president. Looking well, but tiring easily, sitting on

chairs or tables to rest from time to time as she toured the centre, she talked freely about herself, her husband and the expected baby. Charles kept telling her what she should and shouldn't do, she said, and she didn't always like it. 'You don't really know about children until you have them,' one mother advised her. Diana smiled at the woman's twin babies. 'I don't think I could cope with a brace,' she admitted. And she had changed her mind, it seemed, about not minding whether her own baby was a boy or a girl. 'A boy, I hope, but we'll have to wait and see.'

The visit to Deptford was to be her last official engagement before the birth of the baby, but not her last public appearance. Looking the picture of health, though suffering at times from slight backache, she went to Smith's Lawn to watch her husband play polo and she was with him and other members of the Royal Family for the racing at Royal Ascot. She was mainly cheerful, always natural—wearing one of her husband's woolly sweaters when her own became too tight for her because of pregnancy; rebuking a photographer when he pushed a small boy out of the way in an attempt to get a picture of her; rewarding Charles with a kiss when his team won at polo; kissing and cuddling him as they sat together in the royal box at Ascot.

Of the two, it was Charles who became the edgier as pregnancy entered its final phase. 'Mind your own business,' he snapped at a reporter who asked him where the Princess was. Perhaps the fact that it was a reporter who posed the question had something to do with his sharpness on that occasion. He was more forthcoming to an old-age pensioner who asked him how his wife was. 'She is very well, but very hot,' he told her. That was in Battersea Park where he attended a 'Venture Day' organized by Capital Radio. His personal venture that day was to ride from one stand to another as one of a team on a bicycle built for three. It reminded him of a four-seater on which he used to pedal around when he was a schoolboy at Gordonstoun, he recalled.

The fighting in the Falklands had been over for a week when Charles, wearing the uniform of the Parachute Regiment of which he is Colonel-in-Chief, crossed the Channel by helicopter to attend a ceremony commemorating the fortieth anniversary of the war-time raid on Bruneval which had been planned by his murdered great-uncle, Earl Mountbatten. His speech at the ceremony linked past and present together, remembering not only those who had died at Bruneval in 1942 but also those who had lost their lives in the more recent struggle to regain the Falklands.

'When this event was planned,' he said, 'little did any of us know that both the 2nd and 3rd battalions of the Parachute Regiment would be involved in a conflict eight thousand miles away in the South Atlantic, covering themselves in glory and living up to those legendary traditions prized by their predecessors forty years ago.

'We have learned that, while peace is a precious commodity, it cannot conceivably be guaranteed by compromising the values that have been hard fought for and won by the British people over many centuries. That is a recipe for disaster and merely serves to encourage those of a bullying nature who scorn the civilized patterns of behaviour because it is convenient to do so.'

Charles, when he flew to France that day, had left Diana at Highgrove. He would be playing polo at Windsor when he got back, he told her as he left.

But while he was making his speech in France, things were happening back home which were to cause him to change his plans. Despite the earlier forecast that the baby would be born on or about 1 July, Diana's own body now told her that it would be much sooner. Wisely, to be closer to the hospital when the time came, she decided, in her husband's absence, to travel from their home at Highgrove to their apartment at Kensington Palace. So there was to be no polo for Charles that day. Instead, returning from Bruneval, he dashed straight to Kensington Palace to be with his wife.

6 To Diana—A Son

It was around half-past four on the morning of 21 June, 1982 that Diana awoke to the certain knowledge that her baby would be born within a matter of hours. She and Charles dressed, and he helped her into a car and drove her to St Mary's Hospital. At that hour of the morning, with hardly any other traffic about, the trip took no more than a few minutes.

The Praed Street area of Paddington, in which the hospital is located, is hardly the most picturesque part of London. But if the exterior of the hospital seemed drab and unwelcoming, the private room reserved for the Princess on the twelfth floor at a cost of £126.90p. a day provided a relaxing atmosphere of cream-coloured walls and adequate, if plain, furnishings which included a wardrobe and chest-of-drawers, bedside cabinet, telephone and television. For Charles there was an easy chair in which to pass the hours of waiting. He stayed with Diana throughout the sixteen hours she was in labour, which is not an excessive length of time for a young wife having her first child. Suitably gowned, he was with her too for the birth of the baby.

The idea of being with his wife when the baby was born, as his brother-in-law Mark Phillips had been with Princess Anne for the births of their two children, had been in his mind almost since he first knew that Diana was pregnant—which was why, on that visit to Llwynypia Hospital during their tour of Wales, he had asked Shirley Bowen if her husband had been with her. Later he had discussed the idea with George Pinker, the royal gynaecologist, who was very much in favour. 'I think it helps the mother very much,' he told Charles. 'I also believe that it strengthens family bonds.'

It was three minutes past nine that evening when the baby was born, and the controversy over the order of succession to the throne was immediately resolved, at least for the next twenty years or so, when it proved to be a boy. The baby weighed in at 7 pounds 1½ ounces. Thanks to the fact that Diana had diligently performed her pre-natal exercises during her weeks of pregnancy, it was a natural birth or 'very nearly', according to the baby's proud and delighted father.

Whether she knew it or not, Diana had every reason to be thankful that she was a twentieth-century Princess of Wales with none of the problems some of her predecessors had in childbirth, Augusta, the Princess of Wales who was George II's daughter-in-law, was at Hampton Court when she went into labour. To her dismay and distress, her husband, Frederick, determined that the baby should be born at St James's Palace, promptly bundled her into a coach for the twelve-mile drive to London. 'Don't be so silly,' he said, impatiently, in answer to her tearful protests. The journey took them nearly two hours, with the coach bumping and jolting along a road which was little more than a cart-track in places. The wonder was that the baby was not born on the way. As it was, it was ten o'clock at night when they arrived at St James's Palace and the mother-to-be, exhausted and weeping, was helped inside. She was hardly in bed before a baby girl was born.

The Prince of Wales who became King Edward VII at least had the good sense to remain at Frogmore House, Windsor, when his wife, Princess Alexandra, went into labour there some two months before the predicted date. A horse was hastily saddled and a servant galloped into Windsor to fetch the nearest available doctor. He arrived just in time to deliver the baby with the help of the Princess's lady-in-waiting, Lady Macclesfield. It proved to be a tiny mite of only 3 pounds 12 ounces. Its arrival into the world so far ahead of the anticipated date meant that nothing was ready, of course. Lady Macclesfield sacrificed one of her flannel petticoats to serve as a shawl, and a crib was improvised by padding a drawer with cottonwool.

Nor did Diana have to undergo the embarrassing experience of having a representative of the Government present to witness the birth in order to certify that the baby was born in the true line, a practice which started in the seventeenth century after the rumour spread that the baby born to Mary of Modena, second wife of James II, was a changeling smuggled into the royal bedroom in a warming-pan. Queen Victoria, when her turn came, insisted on the Government representative waiting in an ante-room—she was not going to have any strange man watching her give birth—and the Queen's father, King George

VI, after Princess Margaret was born at Glamis with the Home Secretary of the day not arriving on the scene until everything was all over, finally decided to end what he regarded as 'an archaic custom'.

In June 1982 it was necessary only for Prince Charles to telephone the Home Secretary with the news that the Princess had given birth to a son. 'We rejoice with the royal couple,' the Speaker, George Thomas, said in the House of Commons. The official announcement of the birth, signed by George Pinker (it was the eighth royal baby he had delivered), along with David Harvey and John Burton, and posted outside Buckingham Palace, said simply: 'Her Royal Highness The Princess of Wales was safely delivered of a son at 9.03 tonight. Her Royal Highness and child are both doing well.'

Prince Charles, in the words of someone who saw him shortly after the baby was born, was 'absolutely over the moon'. His own words—'relieved . . . delighted . . . over-whelmed'—expressed his feelings. 'You were wonderful, darling,' he told Diana. As well as informing the Home Secretary, he telephoned the news to his parents, to Diana's father, Earl Spencer (who, to be near his daughter on so auspicious an occasion, had journeyed earlier in the day from Althorp to his London flat in Grosvenor Square), and to her mother, the Hon. Mrs Shand-Kydd. The Queen and Prince Philip had spent the day reviewing the RAF Regiment at Wittering, keeping in touch with events through a special radio link. However, they were back home at Buckingham Palace when their son's call came through.

News of the baby's birth was also passed quickly to the grandmothers on both sides, the Queen Mother and her lady-in-waiting, Ruth, Lady Fermoy. 'What lovely news,' Diana's grandmother exclaimed. Word was relayed also to Prince Andrew, at sea aboard HMS *Invincible*. But Princess Anne, who was away in New Mexico at the time, would appear to have received the news after everyone else, judging by what happened when journalists asked what she thought about Diana having a son. 'I didn't know she had had one,' was Anne's reply.

Told that the baby had been born 'this morning'—which was slightly inaccurate even allowing for the difference in time between New Mexico and Greenwich—she said only, 'Oh, good.' It was hardly the sort of joyous reaction the journalists were seeking. 'How do you feel about being an aunt?' they pressed her, hoping for something better.

'That's my business, thank you very much,' the Princess retorted.

It was explained later that she herself did not know that the baby had been born, that she thought the reporters were 'fishing' for information and was correspondingly cautious in what she said, but the episode, seen subsequently by millions on television, was bound to set people talking.

Back in London, flowers for the Princess of Wales had been arriving at St Mary's Hospital throughout the day, and the crowd outside had grown steadily. News of the birth enthused the crowd into noisy snatches of 'Rule Britannia' and 'For He's A Jolly Good Fellow', interspersed with chants of 'It's a boy' and 'We want Charlie.' It was around eleven o'clock that night when they finally got their wish and 'Charlie', beaming a slightly nervous smile, fingering his tie and with a smudge of lipstick on one cheek, emerged from the hospital.

Questions were shot at him thick and fast as the crowd of some three hundred people surged around him.

How did it feel to be a father?

'I'm overwhelmed by it all.'

How were mother and son?

'Doing well. The baby is in marvellous form.'

What was the baby like?

'His hair is fair, blondish, and he has blue eyes. Beautiful.'

Was the baby like its father?

'No, he is lucky enough not to be.'

Like his mother then?

'It's a bit difficult to tell at the moment.'

But the prettiest baby in the world?

'Well, he's not bad.'

Had they decided on a name yet?

'You'd better ask my wife. We've thought of one or two. We've had a little argument about that. We'll find one eventually.'

Some wit in the crowd shouted, 'Nice one, Charlie. Let's have another one.'

'Bloody hell,' returned Charles, grinning. 'Give us a chance. Ask my wife. I don't think she'd be too pleased yet.'

A lot more lipstick was added to the smudge on his cheek as he pushed his way through the crowd towards his car. He grasped a number of outstretched congratulatory hands. 'Thank you; thank you all so very much.'

And finally, easing himself into his car, he appealed to the crowd to quieten down. 'Sleep is badly needed in there,' he told them.

If the royal parents could not as yet agree on a name, the baby at least had a title. Like his father before him, he was born a Prince. Charles, in fact, very nearly missed out on being a Prince from the moment of birth. It was only four days before he was born that his grandfather, King George VI, realized that, as things stood, princely titles could descend only through princely fathers and not through mothers, even if the mother was a princess. He acted quickly to remedy that state of affairs.

Also like his father before him, the as yet unnamed baby was immediately second in line of succession to the throne. Until then, Charles' brother Andrew had been next in line, with Prince Edward following him and then, because boys take precedence over girls, Princess Anne. But now, because the order of succession is vertical in the first instance and horizontal only when it can descend vertically no further, the baby's uncles and aunt had all been pushed back a rung on the succession ladder and might well find themselves going back further in the future if their brother and his wife should have more children.

Genealogists worked out the blood content of the baby Prince who would in due course become Duke of Cornwall, Prince of Wales and Britain's King. Their findings varied slightly, according to how far their calculations went back. One calculated that the baby was 39 per cent English, 16 per cent Scots, 6.25 per cent Irish, 6.25 per cent American with the rest mainly German, while another gave the figures as 57.8 per cent British, 28.12 per cent German, 4.69 per cent American and 4.69 per cent Danish plus a dash of Russian and Polish. Either way, it seemed, he would one day succeed to the throne as the most British monarch since James I (who was 75 per cent Scots) and the most English monarch since Elizabeth I.

Astrologers differed similarly in their perhaps less scientific calculations, one predicting that a baby born under the influence of Cancer would grow up shy, compassionate, intuitive and home-loving, while another forecast that he would be serious and talkative, even argumentative, sometimes

stubborn and sometimes moody. However accurate or otherwise any of this may prove to be, bookmakers at least
seemed endowed with second sight when it came to offering odds
on what name the parents would pick. William and James were
favourites at 7-2, with Charles 9-2, Edward 5-1, Arthur 6-1,
David and Philip each 10-1 and Louis 12-1. It is interesting to
note that one of the two favourites was finally first past the post
and that the three runners-up were all in the betting list.

In London, crowds gathered outside Buckingham Palace as
well as the hospital, celebrating the baby's birth with cheering,
singing and the popping of champagne corks. At Sandringham,
where Diana herself was born, the bells of the parish church
sounded a welcome to the baby, while at Tetbury the ringing of
a handbell brought people into the streets to celebrate.
Congratulatory messages were soon streaming in from all parts
of the world. Robert Muldoon, the New Zealand Prime
Minister, in expressing the 'joy and happiness' of the New
Zealand people, added the hope that the royal couple would
soon visit that country 'and bring your son'. If that tailpiece was
no more than wishful thinking, it was to result in a pleasant
surprise before the baby was a year old. Malcolm Fraser cabled
the congratulations of the Australian people. So did Pierre
Trudeau on behalf of Canada. From America came a message,
to be followed by the gift of a reproduction Chippendale
child's chair, from President and Mrs Reagan: 'Our heartfelt
congratulations on the birth of your son. My wife and I share
your joy. On behalf of the American people we wish him health,
happiness, wisdom and love. We wish you all the pleasures and
joy only a new-born can bring. May God bless and watch over
your family.' In all, more than seven hundred telegrams of
congratulations and good wishes were received overnight,
followed by more than eighteen hundred gifts for the baby
Prince. No one baby could possibly have use for so many
playthings and, generously and charitably, the royal parents
passed most of them on to children's charities and the children's
wards of various hospitals. Diana similarly passed on to hospitals
in and around London many of the scores of bouquets sent to
her, while Charles marked the birth of his son by giving away a
small part of his Duchy of Cornwall holdings. The three
hundred acres of Kit Hill, near Callington, were once the
meeting-place for the ancient Parliament of Tinners of Devon

and Cornwall. To celebrate the baby's birth, Charles gave the hill with its preserved mine stack to the county council for the public.

Inevitably, amidst all the rejoicing over the baby's birth, there was the customary anti-royal remark from William Hamilton, Member of Parliament for Fife Central. The birth of the baby, he was quoted as saying, could only mean 'one long story of nausea and Land of Hope and Glory rubbish for many years'.

Charles was back at the hospital to see his wife and baby son before nine the following morning. He was joined there by a succession of VIP visitors from both sides of the family, Diana's mother and sister, the Hon. Mrs Shand-Kydd and Lady Jane Fellowes; his own mother, the Queen; and Diana's father, Earl Spencer. He left saying that he would look in again later. Between those two visits, eager to keep in touch, he telephoned to talk to his wife.

To his surprise, she told him: 'I want to come home.' She had spoken to her gynaecologist, she said, and he was quite happy for her to do so.

Charles was naturally delighted and drove immediately to the hospital to supervise his wife's departure. Before leaving, they thanked all those who had been involved in the baby's delivery, shaking hands with doctors and nurses and handing out signed photographs of themselves as thank-you gifts. There was an excited gasp from the crowd gathered outside the hospital, followed by a great roar of delight, as the couple emerged, the Prince holding his baby son. He looked proud and Diana positively radiant. They paused at the foot of the hospital steps, and Diana took over the baby, with Charles helping mother and son into the waiting car. But by the time they reached Kensington Palace, the baby was back with Papa and, as they drove in through the gates, Charles could not resist holding up the tiny, shawl-wrapped bundle so that the fresh crowd waiting there could get a good, if fleeting, look at the baby.

For the next few days the couple remained at Kensington Palace, with Diana happily taking charge of the baby, and Charles helping out with such things as changing the occasional nappy. Helping out with baby was partly responsible, though heavy traffic was also to blame, for his late arrival to open a new

research laboratory at Beckenham, Kent. 'I also had one or two
other things to contend with which I am delighted to contend
with,' he said in explaining his lateness. 'The birth of our son has
given us both more pleasure than you can imagine. It has made
me incredibly proud and somewhat amazed.' He was rewarded
for opening the laboratory with an assortment of gifts, a cuddly
doll for the baby, an antique feeding-bottle with a built-in
thermometer and some tubes of ointment intended to sooth
baby's bottom in the event of nappy rash!

Members of both families called round to see how baby was
coming along, among them Princess Anne, back now from her
American trip. Another caller was Mrs Joan Webb, the registrar
for the Marylebone area. Prince or not, the birth of the baby had
to be formally registered within the legal time-limit of forty-two
days. Most parents, of course, are required to attend at the
registrar's office. But not Prince Charles. Mrs Webb came
to him. In fact, she came twice. Through some slight
misunderstanding, the royal parents were not there when she
called at Buckingham Palace. However, she tried again five
days later, at Kensington Palace this time, and found Prince
Charles waiting to supply the necessary details and sign the
register.

By that time, he and Diana had resolved their earlier slight
argument over the baby's names. Their final choice was
William Arthur Philip Louis. 'They're our call-sign,' shouted an
excited Don Weir, manager of a local radio station in Wisconsin,
when he heard the news. 'WAPL—we're the only radio station
in the US with that call-sign.' He promptly parcelled up a T-
shirt, a baseball bat and a WAPL car sticker—'It will look great
on the baby's pram'—and mailed them off to Kensington
Palace.

One reason for picking 'William' for the baby's first name, as
Prince Charles told sailors wounded in the Falkland Islands
fighting when he visited the Royal Naval Hospital at Gosport,
was that he himself did not have any close relative of that name.
Diana had originally wanted 'one of the more modern names'.
Oliver is said to have been one of her suggestions, while Charles
would perhaps have preferred the traditional royal name of
George. But if William was a compromise choice, at least it
revived memories of William the Conqueror and other kings.
Certainly it seemed that, for once, the Royal Family had done

something to please their arch-critic, William Hamilton. 'I am sure they had me in mind when they chose it,' he said, perhaps sarcastically. The choice of name genuinely delighted Diana's father. 'It's a very old Spencer name,' he said. Family records reveal that a certain William le Despencer was steward to Henry I. The name continues to crop up at intervals in the Despencer-Spencer line. A William Spencer was knighted by Henry VIII, while another was honoured in turn by both James I and Charles I.

The baby's second name of Arthur has many royal associations, dating back to the legendary days of King Arthur, as well as being one of Charles' own names, while Philip echoes the name of Charles' father, and Louis remembers the murdered great-uncle he looked upon almost as a grandfather. In an attempt to head off any public attempt to call the baby merely 'Bill' or 'Willy', Buckingham Palace was quick to announce that William would be known officially as 'Prince William of Wales without any foreshortening in any way'.

Ten days after William's birth his mother celebrated her twenty-first birthday. To mark the occasion, no fewer than sixteen Commonwealth countries issued special stamps bearing her portrait. That apart, with the birthday coming so closely on the heels of all the excitement over the birth of the baby, it was thought reasonable that the occasion should be celebrated quietly and privately. Charles, in fact, spent part of the day with more of the men who had been wounded in the Falklands, this time at the Queen Elizabeth Memorial Hospital in Woolwich. He chatted with them at length, made jokes about fatherhood and, ignoring the unwritten rule that members of the Royal Family do not give autographs, signed the plaster cast one man was wearing. That particular cast must now surely be a collector's item. Prince Philip also had signed it a few days before.

At Kensington Palace, however, the Princess's birthday was marred by a slight upset. Children of the Pre-School Playgroup Association, of which she had become president a few months earlier, had been given permission to enter the palace grounds and sing 'Happy Birthday'. 'It had been made quite clear that the Princess would be unable to see them,' Buckingham Palace was to say later. In the excitement of the occasion, no one seems to have paid much attention to that. 'We thought she might come to a window. We even hoped for a glimpse of the baby,' said one of the mothers who had organized the sing-song. In the event, she did not appear even at a window, and the playgroup children, having stood in the rain to sing their birthday greetings, went away wet and disappointed.

While Diana remained at home, looking after the baby, Charles spent the following day in Brixton and Croydon, visiting department stores to learn something of how they operated. There were more gifts for him to take home with him, a playsuit and bootees for the baby, and a crystal vase as a birthday present for his wife. In Brixton, at his own request, he also met local community leaders. He was concerned about the previous year's riots in the area, he told them, and anxious to do anything he could to help.

Being a father made him rather more observant of children, it seemed. Leaving one of the stores he visited that day, he spied a baby girl of a few months cradled in the arms of her grandmother. 'I wouldn't mind a little girl like this myself,' he said, pausing to give the baby a cuddle.

With more and more men returning from the Falklands, Charles continued to play his part in welcoming them home. He was at RAF Brize Norton to greet the returning members of 2 and 3 Para, and he landed by helicopter on the deck of the liner *Canberra* as it entered the Solent with its passenger list of returning Royal Marines. 'I am delighted to do something, however small, towards welcoming these people back,' he said. 'They have done the most fantastic job.'

By now, the three of them, Charles, Diana and the baby, had moved from Kensington Palace to Highgrove, their home in the country, where it was quieter, more peaceful. Except for her departure from hospital, Diana had not yet been seen in public since the birth of the baby. She was breast-feeding him, and motherhood completely filled her time. She had put on weight in pregnancy and was keen to regain her figure before resuming royal duties. With this in view, she began to exercise regularly, starting with some light stretching exercise and later moving on to some of her old, more strenuous, dance routines.

Baby William was a month old when he posed with his parents for his first official portrait. The portrait was a photographic one. The photographer was Lord Snowdon, still close to Prince Charles and others of the Royal Family despite his divorce from Princess Margaret. Diana had her hair done in a new, more sophisticated style, and Charles was relaxedly open-necked as, supporting William between them, they formed a family group for a series of official pictures to be released just over a week later, on the couple's first wedding anniversary.

To the great joy of William's great-grandmother, the Queen Mother, they selected her eighty-second birthday, 4 August, for the baby's christening. The ceremony, performed by Dr Robert Runcie, that same Archbishop of Canterbury who had officiated at their wedding service just over a year before, took place in the white and gold Music Room at Buckingham Palace in which Charles had himself been christened. The silver lily font at which the baby was christened has been used for every Royal Family christening since Queen Victoria gave birth to her first child, the daughter who became Empress of Germany and mother of the Kaiser, nearly a century and a half ago. The christening robe of Honiton lace in which William was dressed for the occasion was likewise a family heirloom which has been worn at royal christenings since the days of Queen Victoria. Dr Runcie was assisted at the ceremony by Canon Anthony Caesar, Sub-Dean of the Chapels Royal, and the choirs of those same chapels were accompanied on the grand piano as they sang the hymns 'O Jesus, I have promised' and 'Guide me, O Thou Great Redeemer' as well as an anthem, 'Blessed Jesu! Here we stand', which the Queen's organist, Richard Popplewell, had composed specially for the christening.

The baby's six godparents spanned the generations. There was the young Duchess of Westminster, to whose baby the Princess of Wales had stood as godmother not many months before, and Lord Romsey, grandson of the murdered Mountbatten and a close friend of William's parents. There was the Queen's cousin Princess Alexandra and Lady Susan Hussey, one of the royal ladies-in-waiting. There was ex-King Constantine of Greece and seventy-five-year-old Sir Laurens van der Post, the South African-born author and explorer. Close relatives on both sides of the family were present at the ceremony with the exception of the baby's uncle Andrew, still serving with HMS *Invincible* in the South Atlantic, and his great-aunt Princess Margaret, who was on holiday in Italy.

William behaved well, letting out no more than the smallest

of infant protests as the Archbishop baptized him, saying, 'William Arthur Philip Louis, I baptize you in the name of the Father and of the Son and of the Holy Spirit. Amen.' But later, when the family gathered in the White Drawing Room for a series of photographs to commemorate the occasion, he felt it was time for a feed and announced the fact at the top of his infant lungs. Several members of the family took it in turns to try to soothe him. 'There, there,' said the Queen and the Queen Mother. Prince Charles tried stroking his son's cheek. Princess Anne, whose own son, Peter, had cried loudly throughout his baptism, moved in to help with a few clucking noises. Nothing worked until his mother introduced her little finger into his mouth. Sucking vainly on that kept him too busy to cry. But each time she sought to remove it, he yelled again.

'He's a good speech-maker,' joked William's paternal grandmother, the Queen.

'Yes, he's got a very good pair of lungs,' agreed his great-granny, the Queen Mother.

Diana meets Elizabeth Taylor, starring in *The Little Foxes*, at the Victoria Palace Theatre, London

Diana supports an aching back while chatting to her husband during a break in a game of polo

Colourful carnival atmosphere at Deptford, May 1982, as Diana opens a new community centre: her last public engagement before the birth

Above: The new parents leave
St Mary's Hospital with baby
William, born 21 June 1982

Right: In August 1982 Prince
Charles flew his wife and son from
Gloucestershire to Aberdeen; here he
carries Prince William off the plane

Below: The Christening of Prince
William of Wales. *Left to right,
standing:* Captain Mark Phillips,
Prince Philip, the Hon. Angus
Ogilvy, Queen Anne Marie of
Greece, Princess Alexandra, King
Constantine of Greece, Lady Susan Hussey, Prince Charles, Lord Romsey, the
Duchess of Westminster, Earl Spencer, Ruth Lady Fermoy, Sir Laurens van der
Post, Prince Edward. *Seated:* Princess Anne, the Queen, the Princess of Wales and
Prince William, the Queen Mother, the Hon. Mrs Frances Shand-Kydd

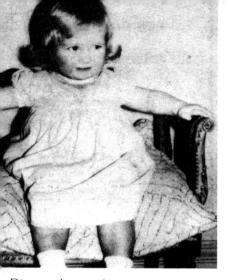

Diana at the age of two

Prince Charles at five months with his mother

Forty-four-day old Prince William after the Christening

Diana visits patients and staff at the Royal Marsden Hospital for Cancer in
Fulham, December 1982

Flashback: Princess Grace of Monaco met Charles and his fiancée Lady Diana Spencer on a visit to London in March 1981

Diana's turquoise dress with diagonal shoulder ruffle was the sensation of a fashion evening at the Guildhall in November 1982: this was the period when she was rumoured to be anorexic

Charles prepares to dive and inspect the wreck of the *Mary Rose* off Southsea for the ninth time; some months later Diana, with director of the investigation Margaret Rule, examines the newly excavated wreck

Huge crowds await the
Prince and Princess of Wales
outside the Sydney Opera
House. The Princess wears
the pink and white flower
dress she wore for her son's
christening

Diana pulls a face during
her husband's speech at the
state reception in Hobart,
Tasmania

Broadcasting on School for the Air throughout the Outback

A moment of relaxation at Ayers Rock

7 Bringing Up Baby

Except for joining with others of the Royal Family in the thanksgiving service which followed the re-taking of the Falkland Islands, Diana devoted almost her whole time to her baby son during the first few all-important months of William's life—and was thrilled to do so. She has doted on children since she was hardly more than a child herself. In schooldays she was like a 'mother' to nervous new girls, one of her teachers recalls. Relatives remember how good she was with smaller cousins when she stayed with them at holiday times. Her first job, after leaving finishing-school, was as a mother's help—she hardly qualified to be called a nanny—with a family living in Hampshire. Later, as the world knows, she taught dancing and painting to the toddlers at a London kindergarten. Now she had a baby of her own to love and care for, and if she did not necessarily do everything exactly as laid down in those books on child upbringing which her husband studied so assiduously, she revealed a sure instinct for the essentials of motherhood, cuddling and playing with William—'I can't stop playing with him,' she confessed to friends—as well as feeding him, bathing him and taking him for regular perambulated outings in the grounds of Highgrove. Prince Charles too was more than happy to undertake his fatherly share of nursery chores, and there was sometimes a laughing altercation between him and Diana as to whose turn it was to bath the baby.

However much the two of them may have differed earlier over the choice of names for their baby son, there was no difference between them (except that Charles would have preferred to 'go by the book' while Diana was content to follow her own instincts) as to how William should be raised. That he should be constantly surrounded by the warmth of parental love came naturally to both of them. If, as he grew older, they were both inclined to spoil him, they were resolved not to molly-coddle him. Almost from the start William came to know a healthy outdoor life, spending long hours in the open air asleep in his baby-carriage. The fact that they did not molly-coddle him does not imply any lack of sensible precautions, and they had William immunized against the more dangerous illnesses of childhood. They were agreed too that, until he was of an age to understand his special role in the scheme of things, royal duties would not be permitted to part him from his parents for long periods, as Charles was so often separated from his.

Life in the nursery suite at Highgrove was not necessarily all sweetness and light, and certainly not all peace and quiet. William quickly showed that he was not the same placid, contented baby that his father had been. As Charles himself was fond of telling people, his small son had 'a good pair of lungs', and the noisy protest he set up at the photographic session which followed his christening was to be repeated often in the months to come.

That so much is known about the babyhood of the future King William V is due largely to his parents. 'Delighted' and 'besotted' with him—their own words—they could no more stop talking about him than can most other young parents. The subject of William was constantly on their lips, in conversation with relatives and friends and, a little later, even when chatting with complete strangers met on royal walkabouts. Of the two, William's proud mother perhaps had most to say about him. The baby had 'bright blue eyes', she said, and 'the most wonderful mass of blond hair'. She did not let him have a dummy to suck. 'He sucks his fingers.' When he was five months old, she proudly announced that he weighed sixteen pounds, already slightly more than double his birthweight. At seven months she confessed, 'He is not crawling yet. But he is quite a handful—fast taking over everything.' Some of her motherly revelations were so frank, indeed, that William, in later years, may find them as embarrassing as others find those nude baby photographs which were once all the rage. Such as the fact that he dribbled rather a lot, and that by five months, as well as more than doubling his birthweight, he had learned the art of spitting. 'It's amazing the things they pick up at his age,' said his mother.

William was not yet two months old when he had his first taste of flying, on a comparatively short hop from London to Balmoral, the first of many similar migrations to which he can look forward in the future—Balmoral in summer, Windsor for

Christmas, Sandringham at the New Year. At first glance, it might seem that the pattern of family life for the Royals has scarcely changed since the turn of the century. But it has, and it is still changing, as that flight to Scotland demonstrated. Because he is heir to the throne, Prince Charles, even in childhood, has never flown on the same aircraft as his mother, the Queen. He has flown with his father, but Prince Philip, of course, is not involved in the line of succession. William is very much involved, as next but one in line. Even so, father and son, mother too, all flew on the same aircraft, William travelling in a carry-cot, and Prince Charles himself acting as pilot.

At Balmoral, that first summer of his life, William and his nanny shared the same nursery suite which Charles and his nanny had once occupied. And the same old-fashioned high pram in which Charles had been wheeled around as a baby was brought out of storage for William's use. The Queen, delighted at finding herself a grandmother again, was happy to share the chore of taking her latest grandchild for an airing in the castle grounds. Members of the family argued, as families will, as to who the baby took after. 'More like Diana than Charles' was the majority opinion, though some thought they also saw a touch of the Mountbattens, transmitted through Prince Charles, if not very much of the Windsors. Princess Anne was at Balmoral at the time with her children, and her small son, Peter, a lively youngster now nearing five, was particularly thrilled with his new cousin and was in and out of William's nursery all the time. And if the baby was sometimes called 'Wills' by his parents, though he was always William to his grandmother, the Queen, Scottish servants at the castle were also quick to coin their own pet name for the latest addition to the Royal Family. Behind royal backs they would refer to him sometimes as 'Wee Willie Wales' after the nursery-rhyme character of somewhat similar name.

If Diana, during those early all-important months of William's life was happier being a mother than a princess, more concerned to be with her baby son than to undertake royal duties, Prince Charles plodded on conscientiously with his share of royal commitments, welcoming yet more troops back from fighting in the Falklands and giving interviews (though barring questions of a personal nature about his wife and son). He would have liked to have remained longer in the Navy if he could have continued flying, he revealed in the course of one interview. But it had become more and more difficult for him. 'People get into a terrible state about flying,' he said. 'You know, if I am going to fly myself into a hill, the sea or whatever.'

He had more to say about his spell in the Navy, and spoke in more lighthearted vein, in the course of another interview, this time on radio. 'My first experience of things like red-light areas came when we had marvellous runs ashore in different places,' he confessed. 'I also met very dangerous sailors who tried to mix your drinks all the time.' He recalled one occasion when he had done a spot of mixing on his own account. It happened when he was a sub-lieutenant on a two-week catering course, and he came up with his own brand of bread-and-butter pudding for the ship's company. 'It happens to be my only speciality. I add all sorts of terrible things like treacle and bananas and brandy. All the sailors kept coming past the galley and saying, "What's that, sir? You can't possibly . . . Yuk!" But afterwards they all thought it was marvellous. They all came back saying, "Cor, that was fantastic. What did you put in it?"'

In more serious vein, he said that, although there were some things he had not liked about life in the Navy—getting up at four in the morning to go on watch was one of them, he thought it 'an important part of life being made to do a certain number of things you don't want to do'. And those night-time watches had also had their advantages. 'If there was nothing much going on, I used to have marvellous talks with the sailors and find out a lot about their lives. What I thought most useful and enjoyable about the Navy for someone like me was the opportunity to meet so many people from all walks of life. It would be difficult for me to meet so many people otherwise. It's not so easy to go and work in a factory, for instance, or down a coal mine, as some people have suggested I should do.'

A doting father though he now was, the Prince continued to be an attentive and affectionate husband also. During a visit to the Highland Games at Braemar in the course of their stay at Balmoral, oblivious of the people more concerned to watch him and Diana than the hammer-throwing and caber-tossing, he took her hand in his, raised it to his lips and kissed it. He accompanied her to London when she journeyed south to attend the wedding to William Bartholemew of Carolyn Pride, one of the three girls who had shared her London flat, and the secret of

Charles' wooing, in courtship days. For Diana, the wedding proved to be something of an old girls' reunion, with her other two former flatmates, Ann Bolton and Virginia Pitman, also among the guests. However, there was little chance to indulge in reminiscences or catch up on news. Anxious to get back to their baby son at Balmoral, the royal couple did not stay for the reception which followed the wedding ceremony.

In Scotland there was some natural degree of disappointment that the Princess, pre-occupied with her baby as she was, did not accept any of the invitations which were extended to the couple during their stay at Balmoral. Charles did accept an invitation to the gala re-opening of the local theatre in Aberdeen, but Diana did not accompany him. The Braemar Games apart, the Princess was seen in public only by those who flocked to watch the Royal Family attend morning service at Crathie on Sundays or by anyone who chanced to be in nearby Ballater on the rare occasion that she went shopping there. There was one occasion when, looking far from her elegant public self, she drove into Ballater to buy one or two things she required from the local chemist and newsagent. As it happened, the sportswear shop had a sale on at the time. So she popped in there too.

The wedding she had attended in London had been very much a private engagement, and the Braemar Games no more than semi-official. Except for the Falklands thanksgiving service, her first official engagement since the birth of the baby was not to have been until late October, a classical concert at the Barbican. However, the sudden and tragic death of Princess Grace of Monaco in a car accident was to alter things. It was necessary for someone to represent the Queen at the funeral service in Monaco Cathedral. With Prince Charles already committed to two engagements in Aberdeen, one of them ending too late at night for him to reach Monaco in time for the funeral, Diana volunteered. She had met the American-born princess at a reception in London shortly after her betrothal to Prince Charles, and much as she disliked the idea of leaving William, the first time she had been away from him overnight, it was something she felt she should do, she said.

Royal engagements are not all concerts and charity film shows, bunfights and beanfeasts. There is also the sad and serious side. For Prince Charles, there was the equally sad and moving experience of a journey to Aldershot to attend an open-air memorial service for the forty-four men of the Parachute Regiment who had died in the Falklands campaign. Wearing the uniform and red beret of the regiment, of which he is Colonel-in-Chief, he read the lesson at the memorial service and took the salute as those who had survived the brief but bitter fighting in the Falklands marched through the town. Afterwards, in the privacy of a convenient hall, he talked with the families of those who had died at Goose Green, Mount Longdon and Wireless Ridge, among them the widow of Lieutenant-Colonel Herbert Jones—'Colonel H'—who was cut down by machine-gun bullets while leading a charge on the Argentinian positions at Goose Green. Sensitive as he always is to the feelings of others, he became so involved emotionally that he stayed with the bereaved parents, widows and children a full hour longer than had been planned.

The royal couple's visit to the Barbican—for a concert by the Russian cellist Mstislav Rostropovich and the English Chamber Orchestra—was also the eve of separation. That separation was, however, a brief and amicable one, occasioned by a five-day visit Prince Charles was paying to the United States and Canada. In part, for him, it was by way of being something of a sentimental journey or, if not that, at least something he felt he owed to his murdered great-uncle, Mountbatten of Burma.

In the evening of his life it had been Earl Mountbatten's ambition to see the growing chain of United World Colleges, of which he was president before handing over to Prince Charles, extended to the United States. Suddenly, a chance meeting between the Prince and Dr Armand Hammer, chairman of Occidental Petroleum, on—of all places—an oil rig in the North Sea, had seen Mountbatten's dream brought to the verge of realization. Subsequent meetings in which Earl Mountbatten took part resulted in Dr Hammer's donating $6 million to build a college in America to go with those already existing in Wales, Canada, Singapore and Swaziland and others planned for Italy, Venezuela and India. But before the project could be completed, Mountbatten was dead, murdered by the IRA, and it was left to his great-nephew Charles to travel alone to Montezuma in New Mexico to perform the opening ceremony.

The United World Colleges aim at promoting peace and international understanding through education, and, as the Prince said in his opening address, 'to encourage the development of self-reliant men and women who are able to take the initiative when necessary and who have the moral courage to stand up for those qualities of human decency and integrity which matter so much'. He did not claim, he said, that the handful of existing colleges would have a dramatic effect on international under-standing. 'Nor is it necessarily going to reduce the chance of armed conflict between nations. But no one who leaves one of these colleges can claim that he or she has not been made aware of the fundamental problems that face mankind and the conditions which can arise to cause misunderstanding and conflict.'

Because of the murdered Mountbatten's link with the project, it was perhaps inevitable that the Irish problem should have been raised by those in America who talked to the Prince on the occasion of the opening ceremony. 'I think it is very difficult for anybody to do anything about the bloodshed in Ireland,' he told those who brought up the subject. 'It's a product of history and people tend to live out their historical characteristics in contemporary existence. So many people have tried to find a solution, but so far it has defeated generations of politicians and well-meaning people. The trouble is that each new generation seems to become infected while they are at an impressionable stage in their lives.'

Television interviews he gave while in America were a shade less serious, a good deal livelier. All three of the nation's major television networks went to the expense of flying their top anchor-women, Diane Sawyer (CBS), Jane Pauley (NBC) and Joan Lunden (ABC) all the way to New Mexico for the privilege of having a real live prince on their breakfast television shows. Questions were supposed to be limited to topics connected with the new college, but this ground-rule, Charles quickly discovered, was to be largely disregarded. Questions were fired at him concerning his marriage, his son, the Falklands and brother Andrew (in the news at that time because of his romantic attachment to actress Koo Stark). He fielded most of them with experienced ease.

'William,' he said in answer to Joan Lunden, 'is the greatest possible fun. He's a most enjoyable child, but then one always thinks one's own child is.'

It was Diane Sawyer who raised the subject of Prince Andrew. Had Charles, she asked, ever wished to face a test such as Andrew had done in the Falklands?

'To a certain extent,' Charles replied. 'I would have liked to have felt that I could be tested to what I consider to be one of the limits, which is to face a question of life and death and serving one's own particular country.'

Was there anything else he wanted to say about his brother? Charles sidestepped that one neatly enough. 'What else can I say except that he's a jolly good chap?'

He was asked what he thought had been his biggest challenge. 'I find it quite a challenge being who I am,' he replied.

But what had most tested his own moral courage? 'I don't know,' he said. 'Maybe I haven't got to that stage. I have a feeling that eventually, before long, I may be put into a position where one faces a particular test or whatever, but then the whole of life is really a test, it seems to me.'

While her husband was away in America opening the new college and in Canada, where he visited the Pearson College in Vancouver, Diana journeyed to Wales to attend a charity gala staged by the Welsh National Opera in Cardiff. There, as everywhere she went, it seemed that she simply could not stop talking about the baby. On a subsequent trip to Cirencester, leaving a playgroup she had been visiting, instead of simply getting back into her car, she walked over to a delighted crowd and began telling them all about William. Charles insisted on bathing him all the time, she said. 'We are both besotted with him; very proud of him.' The visit to the playgroup had been made at her own request. It had been planned that she should stay for only half-an-hour, but she became so involved with the children, sitting on the floor to join them in a pretend tea party, blowing bubbles with them and reading them a story that an hour or more slipped by almost unnoticed.

The baby was again a constant source of conversation when, with Charles, she paid another visit to Wales. Wherever they went, Aberdyfi, Machynlleth, Dolgellau, she talked about him all the time. 'He's getting bigger every day; he's getting very heavy.' And the sound of a baby crying somewhere in the crowd saw her tug her husband's sleeve. 'We know all about that, don't we?' Nor was Charles always left behind in all this talk about baby William. 'William is wonderful fun and really makes you laugh,' he told someone in the crowd when the two of them visited Wrexham. 'He's not at all shy. He's a great grinner, but he does dribble a lot.'

'He's just like his father,' interposed Diana, mischievously.

But William was not his father's sole topic of conversation at this time. Another, and perhaps more dominant, subject of princely conversation, if his wife can be believed, was the raising of the *Mary Rose*. 'He talks about it all the time,' Diana said. As president of the Mary Rose Trust, Charles had been on the spot to see Henry VIII's flagship finally and successfully brought to the surface, though not without a few alarums and excursions along the way. So intrigued did Diana become with her husband's frequent references to the project that she decided to see for herself. Accordingly, she paid a visit to Portsmouth dockyard, where she was air-lifted in the bucket of a hydraulic hoist to get a bird's-eye view of the salvaged Tudor warship while archaeologist Margaret Rule pointed out features of interest to her. 'Now I can compete,' said the Princess with evident satisfaction.

8   Press Relations

'Charles stormed out of Kensington Palace on the way to an engagement, slammed the oak door behind him, and she shouted, "Don't you dare go without me".'

That fly-on-the-wall account by an anonymous 'palace insider' of a supposed marital upset was published by a New York periodical for the benefit of its American readers when the royal couple had been married for some eighteen months. 'She', of course, was Diana.

It is one of the penalties of being a superstar, whether film, pop or royal, that you are obliged to endure a non-stop spate of rumour, gossip and speculation about your personal life, much of it exaggerated, some of it with no foundation at all in fact. For Charles and Diana, the rumours started in the first few weeks of marriage, while they were at Balmoral enjoying the holiday which followed their honeymoon cruise. The Princess was not getting along too well with her royal in-laws, one newspaper hinted. Other rumours since have encompassed almost the entire spectrum of their personal life—Diana did not like Highgrove and wanted a bigger place, it was said; she did not like being left alone so much while Charles was off hunting; and he complained that she was spending too much on clothes—and will doubtless continue to do so until they are an old, staid married couple and no longer quite so newsworthy.

They can perhaps draw some small degree of comfort from the fact that Prince Charles' parents, for years, suffered the same sort of thing. American and European publications, in particular, became skilled at depicting their marriage as on the verge of breakdown. Indeed, such rumours were still to be seen in print almost up to the time they celebrated their silver wedding anniversary. Anne and Mark, too, have been forced to endure the same sort of thing over their years of marriage.

It is doubtless true that royal couples, like any ordinary husband and wife, do have their differences of opinion from time to time, their marital tiffs and arguments. They would need to be placid to the point of dullness not to do so. And equally doubtless, as with most ordinary married couples, such small upsets are quickly over and forgotten. Unless, of course, the media latches on to something—a spot of backstairs gossip between servants, something a friend told a friend who told yet another friend and which became distorted in the telling, even the failure to display the expected royal smile on a public occasion. Then the hints, rumour, gossip start yet again.

Prince Charles, during that visit to America when he opened the Armand Hammer United World College of the American West, was asked bluntly on television: 'Who is to blame for Press attention to the recent event [a reference to Prince Andrew and Koo Stark] and reports of conflict in your own marriage?'

If Diana Sawyer of CBS, who posed this blunt question, had expected Charles to give an equally blunt reply, she was due for disappointment. Years of experience have made Charles skilled in the art of handling such tricky and loaded questions. 'You blame the readers who buy the newspapers or viewers who watch the programmes which have them,' he replied, diplomatically and adroitly. However, he also took advantage of his appearance on American breakfast television to explain something of his own attitude to the gossip so constantly published about himself and his wife. 'As I get older, I find less privacy becomes available and more people seem to be interested in every small and minute aspect of one's life. Somehow you have to have the outlook or philosophy which enables you to bear it, otherwise, I promise you, it's very easy to go mad.'

That Charles is able to 'bear it' rather than 'go mad' is due to years of conditioning. Like his father before him, he has perhaps now reached the stage when he can read the things written about him with the same degree of detachment as if he was reading about 'some animal in a zoo'. Diana, coming later and more suddenly to her royal role, can hardly, as yet, have developed the same philosophical outlook. Sensitive as she is, it will take time before she does develop it, and perhaps she never will.

One lesson she learned early on, in courtship days, is that an attempt to 'get the record straight'—her own phrase at the time—can sometimes have the effect of complicating things still further. Such was the case when she granted an interview for the purpose of denying that she had spent the night with Charles aboard the royal train. True, the published interview included her denial: 'The story was completely false. I was not on the royal train when they said and have never been on the royal train.' But it also gave what were said to be her views on marriage: 'I'd like to marry soon. I don't think nineteen is too young. Age doesn't matter.' And more in the same vein. Hardly the remarks calculated to touch off an international incident, but highly embarrassing to a young lady hoping to marry a Prince of Wales who has not yet actually proposed. Diana felt it necessary to issue yet another denial—'It's simply not true. I never said anything about marriage'—while the Press Association, which had circulated the interview, insisted that she had been reported correctly. Since then, though she has appeared at Charles' shoulder for the occasional Press conference, contributing the odd remark, she has declined requests made to interview her personally. But in her own fashion she still attempts to 'get the record straight' when the newspapers are wide of the mark. 'By the way, I am feeling very well,' she told people in Cirencester, for instance, at a time when there were newspaper reports that she was suffering from anorexia nervosa.

The newspaper stories of anorexia nervosa were the product of what happened at the 1982 British Legion Festival of Remembrance at the Albert Hall. This is a function which the Royal Family invariably attends in some strength. So it was perhaps only to be expected that journalists should wonder why Charles arrived without his wife. She was feeling slightly unwell, he was understood to say by way of explanation. That in itself was more than sufficient to ensure newspaper headlines the following day. What happened subsequently made such headlines doubly certain. While attendants were still in the act of removing Diana's chair from the royal box, she appeared belatedly on the scene. It was precisely the sort of small royal incident which many editors, in this day and age, regard as more newsworthy than civil war in Lebanon or a *coup d'état* in Central America. As the Queen's Press secretary, Michael Shea, was to put it: 'A new wave of hysteria has gripped the more sensational Press. Anything to do with any aspect of the Royal Family, no matter how minute, is treated as a huge news story.' The story of Diana's belated arrival at the Albert Hall was certainly given that sort of treatment by many newspapers, with the incident reported in elaborate detail and all manner of theories trotted out to account for what had happened. Charles and Diana had had a tiff and she had refused to accompany him, but later thought better of it. So ran one theory. It was her health, another newspaper theorized; she was suffering from post-natal depression, and public life was proving too much of a strain so soon after childbirth. Either that or she was dieting too much. Lending support to this second theory was Diana's appearance since she had again been seen in public. Gone was the chubby teenage look of early marriage. Dieting to regain her figure following the birth of the baby had made her slim in the extreme. Was she perhaps suffering from anorexia nervosa, the slimming disease for which one of her sisters had once been treated, some newspapers wondered.

Buckingham Palace was bombarded with questions aimed at eliciting further details. Was the Princess about to cancel her engagements? Certainly not, said the palace. 'She is looking fit and well and has been in sparkling form. She has been appearing regularly in public, and people can judge for themselves. If there was anything wrong, she would not be making these personal appearances.'

Relatives and friends of the Princess similarly found themselves again being sought out by reporters as they had not been since her courtship days. They all gave much the same answer. Rumours of ill-health were simply not true. Diana was fit and well—a healthy young wife and mother. One of those questioned did, however, add a small rider. One thing was upsetting her—all this exaggerated speculation about her health.

But the newspapers, having got the bit between their teeth, were reluctant to give up galloping. Speculation continued despite all the denials, official and unofficial. Nor were the stories of Diana's supposed ill-health entirely ended even when she appeared again in public the following day, in Whitehall for the annual Remembrance Day ceremony at the Cenotaph and at Wellington Barracks, later, for the Welsh Guards service. Remembrance Day, that year, coincided with Charles' thirty-fourth birthday, a fact which brought an outburst of 'Happy Birthday' from the crowd, with Charles and Diana smiling and waving happily as they drove off again in the direction of Kensington Palace.

It was to require yet another public appearance on Diana's

part before the newspapers would finally cease speculating about her health. With other members of the Royal Family she made the short trip to Westminster Pier to welcome Queen Beatrix of the Netherlands and her husband, Prince Claus, at the start of their four-day state visit to London. She looked fit enough, well enough, if on the slim side. And if it was a marital tiff rather than ill-health which had been the cause of her late arrival at the Albert Hall, that was all over and forgotten, as was clearly seen when Prince Charles, having escorted the Dutch visitors up-river in the royal barge, nipped quickly down the gangplank to slip an affectionate arm around his wife's trim waist.

Charles had, in fact, a special reason to be pleased for and proud of his wife that day. In a small private ceremony his mother had given the Princess a miniature portrait in the form of a brooch. These brooch miniatures of the Sovereign constitute a Royal Family Order which the Queen awards to female relatives who have won their spurs, so to speak, on the field of public appearances.

But the newspapers had not yet finished with the Prince and his wife. Before the month was out, another story of supposed marital disharmony had appeared in at least one newspaper. This time it hinged on the fact that Charles had taken to hunting more or less regularly with the Quorn in Leicestershire. Diana, so the story ran, had no interest in her husband's sporting pursuits, hunting, horses, polo, shooting and fishing. As a result, there was 'tension' between them, a state of affairs which was 'of great concern to the Royal Family'. Maybe. And maybe the story had its origin in a joking remark Charles had made a week or so earlier. Asked by a fellow huntsman how he was enjoying married life, he quipped in reply, 'It's all right, but it interferes with my hunting.'

Since the wedding there had been little or no contact between the parents of bride and groom. However, a royal visit to Northampton was the occasion of a meeting between Charles' mother and Diana's father, who had served as a royal equerry for the first two years of the Queen's reign. He took the opportunity to invite her back to his stately home for tea. As recently as the early part of the Queen's reign it would have been almost unthinkable for her to have accepted such an invitation from a divorced man, however innocent. But times change and the Royal Family is sufficiently alert to change with them. The Queen, in an era which has seen her own sister undergo the trauma of divorce, saw no conceivable way in which the Crown might be tarnished by her accepting Earl Spencer's invitation, and she did.

More and more the youngest of the Earl's three daughters was managing deftly to dovetail her dual, if sometimes conflicting, role of princess and mother. Over a period of some two weeks, as November merged into December that year of 1982, she carried out a busy spate of no fewer than seventeen public engagements, including another two-day tour of her husband's principality. Despite heavy rain—it seemed always to rain when she visited Wales—she insisted upon the now traditional walkabouts. Elsewhere, a typical working day saw her board a helicopter to fly to Birmingham, where she opened a new children's centre before going on to Coventry to visit a home for old people. Then it was back to London in time to attend a charity concert in the evening. Next day was as busy again, a visit to the Royal Marsden Hospital in Fulham followed by a gala ballet performance at the Royal Opera House in the evening. The day after saw her visiting a playground for handicapped children with a charity film première to follow. No sign of ill-health in all this, though she was in fact recovering from a heavy cold at the time.

Charles has always fancied himself as something of an actor. As a schoolboy at Gordonstoun he played the title role in Shakespeare's *Macbeth* and that of the Pirate King in *The Pirates of Penzance*. But it was at Cambridge that his gifts of mimicry and comic inventiveness really came into their own, with his appearances in a multitude of roles in two student revues. He enjoys making 'a legitimate fool' of himself, he has said. 'I love it. It helps to keep me sane.' Since leaving Cambridge, opportunities to make a legitimate fool of himself have tended to be conspicuous by their absence. However, the gala evening at the Royal Opera House, which he and Diana attended, offered an opportunity too good to miss. Prancing unannounced onto the stage in tights and cloak, he proceeded to play a mock and unrehearsed *Romeo and Juliet* scene with his wife seated in the royal box.

'Speak to me, speak to me,' he pleaded in tones of mock passion.

If his appearance came as a complete surprise to the audience, Diana at least was quick to enter into the spirit of the occasion. 'Just one cornetto,' she sang back at him, echoing the words of a well-known television jingle. Thereupon Charles dashed off-stage, returning with a ladder which he propped against the royal box, clambering up it to kiss his wife's hand while the audience applauded enthusiastically.

But the royal round is by no means all fun and games. It has its more serious, even sadder, moments. Sensitive as the Princess is, her visit to the Royal Marsden Hospital must have been a stressful experience for her. Not only is it a leading cancer hospital, but the one in which her young cousin Conway Seymour had died only two years before. She was among the first to support a fund to her cousin's memory which his mother launched with the object of providing the hospital with new equipment. Now, with the new equipment bought and installed, it was at her own wish that she visited the hospital, pausing to chat cheerfully with several of the patients.

Equally for Prince Charles, who is more tender-hearted than his addiction to hunting and shooting would suggest, it was an emotional experience, as Colonel-in-Chief of the Cheshire Regiment, to journey to Chester for a memorial service to the ten men of the regiment who had been killed by a bomb blast in Northern Ireland. Nor did he leave immediately after the service, but stayed on to offer what words of comfort he could to the grieving relatives of the dead men.

More and more, these days, the royal round tends to bring its stars into contact with the harsh realities of everyday life. Charles, for instance, saw something of life on the dole when he visited Consett, that once thriving steel town which recession had turned into one of Britain's worst unemployment blackspots. However, his visit, to a new industrial development on the site of the old steelworks, perhaps sounded a small note of hope for the future. Diana, because her upbringing was very different from that of her princely husband, far less cocooned, can be expected to know more about the realities of life. So it perhaps came as no surprise to her, on one of the many public engagements she carried out around this time, to find her way barred by a picket of protesting civil servants. Fortunately, a quiet chat between police and protesters saw her able to proceed without further let or hindrance.

Royal visits are always carefully planned, meticulously arranged, delicately timed. Even so, things can go wrong; the unexpected can happen—as when Charles and Diana journeyed to Merseyside for the launching of a canal boat intended to provide trips for handicapped children. Diana was to perform the launching ceremony. She duly named the boat *Pride of Sefton*, whacked the obligatory bottle of champagne against its bow and began to walk away, only to check herself as she realized that the champagne bottle was unbroken. Blushing, she walked back and tried again. And still the bottle obstinately refused to break. 'I don't think it will ever break,' she murmured to Charles, blushing all the more. Grinning, he lent a hand, and their combined effort finally saw the *Pride of Sefton* well and truly launched.

Baby William was now six months old. Proud as they were, and are, of him, the royal parents arranged a photographic session at Kensington Palace so that the whole world might see how he was coming along. For all that relatives had thought earlier that William was perhaps more like his mother than his father, the photographs taken on that occasion reveal a strong resemblance to Prince Charles when he was around the same age. He had surveyed the world then with a questioning, rather serious look. So did William now. His father felt it necessary to apologize to the assembled photographers for his son's lack of smiles. 'I'm sorry he's not all that smiley today,' he said. 'They never do when you want them to. We'll probably get all those child specialists saying we handled him wrong.' Eventually, however, with the Princess coaxing her baby son with smiles, cuddles, kisses and tickles, William's serious, questioning look dissolved into smiles and chuckles.

William had so far shown himself to be a more demanding baby than his father was at the same age. Charles was quiet and placid as a baby, shy and uncertain as a small boy, frowning more often than he smiled, almost as though (some thought) he could already feel the weight of a future crown upon his young head. It was not until he went to Australia in schooldays that he began to shed his inhibitions and, in his own words, 'come out of my shell'. That shell was to disappear completely during the years he was at university and at sea with the Royal Navy. But in more recent years, despite the playboy label pinned on him by the Press, there has been perhaps a tendency to regress. He might have developed into something of a crusty bachelor had Diana not come into his life. Marriage and fatherhood have combined to change him yet again. An unnamed member of his staff has been quoted by an American magazine as saying: 'Since the Prince fell in love with Diana and they have had Prince William, he has become a much more warm and open person.' That anonymous quote, for once, has a ring of truth.

The same unnamed source has been further quoted as saying: 'Prince William has brought them close together. They are very much in love and don't care who knows it. They are openly affectionate in the privacy of their own apartments.' And not only in the privacy of their own apartments. In public too they have constantly been seen holding hands, cuddling, even kissing upon occasion.

If that pre-Christmas photo-call was intended as a sop to Cerberus, a gesture extended to Fleet Street in the hope of being permitted privacy over Christmas and the New Year, it did not work. Those pictures of Prince William served to whet rather than satisfy editorial appetites, and some fifty reporters and photographers were to be found camping out at Sandringham when the couple joined the Queen there for the New Year, following the Royals everywhere they conceivably could without actually trespassing. It was the worst New Year ever at Sandringham, the Queen said at one point. In Liechtenstein, a few days later, things were to become even worse, however, with the love-hate relationship between palace and Press reaching a new low ebb.

Newspapers and, to a lesser extent, television have arrived at a point where the Royal Family is treated as one long true-to-life serial story. Even as this is being written, there are, in one newspaper and on a single day, no fewer than four stories about various members of the family: Charles playing polo, Andrew slipping away to some unknown destination, Edward joining the Royal Marines and the Duchess of Kent planning a return to the royal round after a period of ill-health.

In an era when the effect of Diana's arrival on the scene has been to turn almost the whole British nation, with the exception of a few like William Hamilton, into a tribe of royalty-worshippers, it is of course good for circulation. Because it is good for circulation, editors are bound to seek more and more stories and photographs about the cult-figures of the age. In doing so, it is inevitable that what is written should sometimes be inaccurate, exaggerated, even invented, if not by those who do the writing then by those who supply the raw material. It is perhaps inevitable too that photographers, in their desire to obtain that one picture that will go round the world, should sometimes venture beyond that invisible and ill-defined line which separates the permissible from the private. Trespass is defended on the grounds that it is accidental, inaccuracies on the pressure of newspaper deadlines, and both on the assumption that the Royal Family depends on publicity for its popularity.

The assumption is ill-founded. The Queen's father, grandfather and great-grandfather, even her great-great-grandmother, Queen Victoria, were all popular with the public of their day though television did not exist and newspapers were a good deal more in awe of the Royal Family than they are today. Prince Charles, on American television, blamed those who read newspapers and those who watch television for today's changed state of affairs. But the desire of those who run newspapers and television for bigger circulations and larger viewing figures is also to blame. So, too, is the Royal Family itself and those whose duty it is to advise them on such matters. You can hardly expect to be lauded like a pop star in public one minute and have your privacy respected as a member of the Royal Family the next—as Charles and Diana were to discover afresh when they flew to Liechtenstein that winter for the ten-day skiing holiday originally planned for the previous year and then abandoned when Diana realized that she was pregnant.

They did not take William with them, devoted as they were to him, but left him at Sandringham in the care of Nanny Barnes, with his royal grandmother to keep a supervisory eye on things. With an eye to privacy, they had arranged to stay in the castle home of Prince Hans Adam, whose family are long-time friends of the Royal Family. Situated near Vorab, it would serve as a vantage-point from which they could journey easily to several different snow slopes.

To their dismay, they arrived at Vaduz, the Liechtenstein capital, to be greeted by even more photographers and reporters than there had been at Sandringham. British and European, there were so many of them that the hotel next door to their holiday home castle almost bulged at the seams. On their very first day out on the ski slopes a helicopter hired by a contingent of Swiss photographers leap-frogged ahead of them in an attempt to obtain pictures of Diana as she slalomed downhill in a striking red ski-suit. Not unnaturally, her skiing suffered. Upset and annoyed, she retreated to a mountain restaurant and sat forlornly in a room set aside for her use while her husband continued to ski on his own. The photographers were still around when he eventually rejoined her. To escape their attentions, the royal couple ducked out of the restaurant by way of the kitchens and took off unobserved down a convenient snow slope.

The following day they drove into Austria to ski at St Christoph, dodging the photographers. The third day found them again in Austria, this time at Zurs. Prince Charles, one newspaper reported, 'always tries as many different slopes as he can in order to make his skiing as varied and exciting as possible'. The constant changes of venue, in fact, were as much to dodge the Press as to vary the skiing. To an extent, such ploys were successful. 'Well, I'm glad there were no photographers around to take pictures of that,' said Diana on one occasion when she came a cropper.

To aid them in their attempts to avoid the Press, the local police co-operated with the couple's personal detective, Superintendent John Maclean, to the extent of setting up a system of road-blocks and pass-checking. Not unnaturally, the pressmen not only objected but sought to avoid such not-strictly-legal restrictions. They endeavoured to pursue the royal couple in cars and on skis while the police, in turn, pursued them. An increasingly ugly situation developed in which Press cars were run off the road, a photographer was struck by one of the local police and a skiing correspondent accused Superintendent Maclean of knocking him over on the edge of a 300-foot drop.

With the situation becoming more heated almost by the minute, two of the Prince's aides, his assistant private secretary Francis Cornish and his Press secretary Victor Chapman, flew to Liechtenstein in an attempt to pour oil on troubled ski slopes. Members of the British Press contingent were, they found, inclined to blame Diana for the situation which had arisen, accusing her of being 'unco-operative'. On the rare occasions that such awkward situations arise between the Royals and the Press, a compromise is usually possible. The Royals agree to pose for a few pictures and answer a few questions, as Charles and Diana had done at Balmoral in the aftermath of their Mediterranean honeymoon, in return for being left in peace subsequently. But not this time. 'All we wanted was a few minutes in the morning,' the pressmen told Cornish and Chapman. 'A few smiles from the Princess and there would have been smiles all round.' But Diana, for once, refused to oblige. Charles himself had already tried to persuade her, but with little success. Her answer had been to appear with her hat pulled down almost over her eyes and her face buried in her upturned collar, which was hardly what the photographers wanted. Now Cornish and Chapman added their pleas to those of her husband. In vain. Upset at not being permitted to enjoy her holiday in private, and perhaps still smarting over those bikini photographs taken when she was last on holiday, doggedly she maintained her refusal to pose for the photographers. In any event, as she pointed out, there was no guarantee that European photographers would leave her in peace afterwards even if the British contingent did. And perhaps she was right. The possibility of obtaining a picture of the Princess of Wales on her *derrière* was perhaps too great a temptation. Her continued refusal to co-operate resulted in stalemate. Any request to recall their teams could be made only to British editors; so none was made. However, with royal displeasure so patently obvious, editors in Britain began withdrawing their photographers and reporters of their own accord. But by then the holiday was half over and the problem of the European pressmen still remained.

Ruined though her holiday had been to a large extent, upset and obstinate though she was at the time, it was the Diana people have come to know and love who resumed public duty on the couple's return to Britain, donning a striking blue and green outfit to smile at the cameras, if not the cameramen, when she and Charles attended the opening ceremony of the 'Britain Salutes New York' Festival at the Royal Academy. But she turned down an invitation to present the British Press Awards later that year—though this, it was hastily explained, had nothing to do with what had gone before. She and Charles would be away in Australia and New Zealand at the time the awards were due to be presented, it was stated.

9 Fashion Note

People who saw the Prince and Princess on one or other of the many outdoor engagements they undertook during the bitterly cold winter weather of 1982-3 were sometimes puzzled, even concerned, by the comparatively light outfits Diana so often wore, a woollen two-piece perhaps or even a silk dress more suited to the warmer weather of spring or summer than the chill of winter. She had to be a lot hardier than her appearance suggested, they mused. Even so, wasn't it taking a risk? A jesting remark by the Princess herself, let slip in the course of a visit to an adventure playground in south-east London, revealed the secret of how she manages to wear such light clothing and still keep warm in bad weather. 'I'm a walking advertisement for Damart,' she said. Damart, for the benefit of those who do not attempt to scale Everest or explore the Arctic, are the makers of thermal underwear.

But Diana has become more than merely 'a walking advertisement for Damart' since marrying the Prince of Wales and emerging upon the public scene as a member of the Royal Family. More importantly, she has shown herself to be a living, breathing advertisement for the whole of Britain's fashion trade. Not since the Duke of Kent's mother, the elegant Princess Marina, stunned Britain with her eye-catching clothes back in the 1930s has there been a royal princess with such a flair for and delight in clothes.

Like the late Princess Marina, the present Princess of Wales has the physical attributes—height and figure—to display clothes to perfection. At 5 feet 10 inches, slim-built with long legs, had she been so inclined, she would have made an ideal professional model. Her life-style suggests a determination to preserve her model-girl figure. She does not eat breakfast, she says. She takes her tea without either milk or sugar. She is aware of and careful to avoid the dangers which lurk on the production line of luncheons, dinners and banquets which forms a not inconsiderable part of the royal working environment. For her it was salad instead of tenderloin pork at a Duchy of Cornwall lunch in Devon—'I have to watch my waistline,' she said—and salmon instead of an outsize steak at a barbecue, later, in Canada. In Grimsby, visiting a hospital, she declined even 'a nibble' of the lavish buffet which had been prepared. 'I don't think so,' she said. 'It will spoil my figure.' While remarks about 'waistline' or 'figure' are made lightly, even jestingly, she is serious enough about it all.

With Britain in the throes of recession, the boost the Princess has given the fashion trade could hardly have come at a more opportune time. In the six months following the royal wedding, more than two hundred copies of her elaborate wedding-dress were sold by one firm alone. Oddly, Arab brides from the Middle East were among the main buyers. Knickerbockers, culottes and capes have all become fresh fashions in turn as the Princess set the trend. Equally, seen out and about in a seemingly endless succession of nifty boaters and dainty pillboxes, dashing tricornes and shadowy sombreros, she has been 'good news for the hat trade', according to John Boyd, one of those who design for her. Copies of the rakish tricorne which formed part of her going-away outfit were still selling well a full eighteen months after the wedding, while hat-makers generally reported a twenty per cent increase in sales as other girls copied Diana. Indeed, one firm in Luton, that home of hat-making, reported a fifty per cent jump in sales to five thousand hats a week. Diana has a particular penchant for hats with misty veils, but these, while adding an air of romantic mystery, can cause the occasional problem for someone whose public duties take her so often among children. A three-year-old in one hospital she visited, in Wrexham, was so intrigued that he clutched the veil and tugged hard. Only quick action on the part of the Princess prevented her from parting company with her hat.

That the Princess should have become such a trend-setter is perhaps remarkable in a young woman who, as a bachelor girl, according to friends, went about mostly bare-headed and had no particular interest in clothes. With one exception. 'Her skiing outfits—they were always stunning,' one friend recalls. 'But for the rest, she wasn't much bothered. Often she wore just jeans and baggy sweaters.'

Relaxing at Highgrove or Balmoral, even shopping in

Tetbury or Ballater, the Princess is still happy to wear, if not
exactly 'jeans and baggy sweaters', at least their casual equivalent.
But in other respects the teenaged chrysalis has metamorphosed
into a royal butterfly, and the clothes she wears for public
engagements are mostly, though perhaps not always, as
'stunning' as her ski outfits were and still are. Since marrying
Charles she has spent what, to an ordinary girl, would be a small
fortune on clothes from some of the country's leading designers
. . . tailored suits by Joseph Conran, day dresses from Jan
Vanvelden, evening dresses by Gina Fratini. The fashion
house of Belville Sassoon has been among her favourites
since designing her going-away outfit and others she favours
include Benny Ong, Bruce Oldfield, Arabella Pollen and
Caroline Charles. However, not all her clothes are individually
created for her. For leisure outfits she is also known to patronize
an up-market chain store from time to time.

For special occasions she has a happy knack of suiting her
clothes to the occasion, devising that little extra touch which
seems to echo the mood of the moment: an outfit in red and
green, the Welsh national colours, for her first sortie into Wales;
red and white, the colours of the Canadian flag, on her first day
in Canada; a full-length white gown with a modest V-neck plus
a tiara and pearls the first time she attended the State Opening
of Parliament; black with a youthful froth of lace at the throat
and wrists for a Remembrance Day service at the Cenotaph. She
has developed a deft touch for wearing not only what best suits
her tall, slim figure, but also what emphasizes her vibrant,
romantic personality: a belted Cossack-style coat with matching
hat and muff for a winter visit to Gloucester Cathedral; a velvet
suit in midnight blue to switch on the Christmas lights in
London's Regent Street; a flowing full-length evening cape for
dinner at the Houses of Parliament.

For all this, those who design for her tend to give her most of
the credit. 'She has her own ideas,' they say. 'She is very positive
about what she wants.' Whoever truly deserves the credit—the
Princess herself, her designers or, most probably, both—it is
undeniably her evening gowns which are the most eye-catching.
Perhaps the most striking was that strapless Scarlett O'Hara
creation in black silk taffeta which she wore when she
accompanied her husband-to-be to the Royal Opera House on
her first-ever public engagement. Charles, that evening, could

scarcely take his eyes from her. But if there has been nothing quite so sensational since, there has been spectacle enough to provoke gasps of admiration, delight and possibly envy: a slim-fitting blue silk dress with a one-shoulder neckline for a fashion show at London's Guildhall; a striking black and burgundy creation for the London première of *E.T.*, while later, 'Down Under', it was to be red silk spotted with silver for a state ball in Tasmania and blue chiffon streaked with silver thread for a charity function in Sydney. And topping everything else she was to wear in Australia and New Zealand was that dramatically figure-hugging, one-shoulder creation in white silk crêpe which she wore for the farewell ball in Melbourne.

Australian fashion experts certainly had no cause to criticize her evening gowns, whatever they might find to say about her daytime outfits. And they found plenty. 'Plain Jane-ish' one fashion critic labelled them. 'Are Diana's Clothes Too Matronly?' queried a headline. 'Let's See More Of Your Lovely Legs, Diana,' urged another. 'Although the fashionable skirt length in London is presently longer than in Sydney,' explained one commentator, 'the mid-calf dresses with flattish shoes Diana favours can sometimes look a little off the mark.' Fashion designers in Canada, when she and Charles went there later, were inclined to be similarly critical. Said one, Gerald Franklin: 'She should dress more like a princess, with more opulence in her clothes. Right now she is not reflecting any image and has not found any personal style.'

Two points were overlooked by the Australian critics at least. The Princess is a tall young woman. At 5 feet 10 inches, she is only an inch shorter than her husband. The 'flattish shoes Diana favours' are necessary if she is not to tower over him on public occasions. Imagine the effect if she wore four- or five-inch heels plus an ostrich-feathered hat! And mid-calf dresses serve a more important function than simply echoing 'the fashionable skirt length in London'. On walkabouts they also have the important advantage of preserving modesty when the Princess stoops or crouches, as she often does when talking to children or disabled people confined to wheelchairs. Shorter dresses on such occasions might reveal a little too much of her 'lovely legs' and provide accompanying photographers with something of a field day.

In any event, whatever Australian fashion critics and

Canadian designers may have had cause to think, as far as the
average Australian or Canadian was concerned she could have
worn an old potato sack and still have looked fabulous.

Her appeal to the public is not a matter of what she wears.
Nor is it due entirely to her physical appearance, attractive
though she undoubtedly is. It is not simply sex appeal, for the
aura she projects cuts across the boundaries of sex and age alike,
fascinating women perhaps even more than men, the very
young as well as the very old and those of all ages in between.
Nor is it due to the age-old mystique of royalty, though that is a
contributory factor. The charisma she exudes is a combination
of all these things in varying degrees plus an X factor which is
peculiarly her own.

On her first tour of Wales, people had sought to touch her as
though some of her magic might rub off on them. A year and a
bit later, the magic (if that is what it is) was still there, stronger
than ever. And it was to be stronger still in the months ahead, on
her visits with Charles to Australia, New Zealand, Canada,
until at times what was to become known as 'Dimania'
threatened to get entirely out of hand. In Australia they would
compare it with the Beatlemania of the 1960s, but the
comparison is not strictly valid, for she does not sway the crowds
with music as the Beatles did. She does not dance or sing—at
least not in public—nor resort to oratory. She leaves the speech-
making to her husband. She simply walks and talks, smiles,
blushes occasionally and shakes a multitude of hands. So what is
it that draws people to her presence in such vast numbers?
Scientists cannot analyse it, though psychologists have tried.

In Bristol, when she went there in February 1983, as in Wales
in October 1981, her path was strewn with flowers, so many that
the point was reached where her lady-in-waiting could no
longer cope and Sir John Wills, Lord Lieutenant of Avon, was
obliged to lend a hand. And even this was merely a foretaste of
what lay ahead of her in Australia and New Zealand, where she
was to be inundated with so many flowers that whole teams of
helpers would be required to carry them away. In Bristol, as
elsewhere, many of the offerings were humble posies tendered by
small children. 'Don't suck your thumb or your teeth will fall
out,' the Princess smilingly cautioned one small girl. If that was
true, William would probably never have had any teeth and by
now, to the delight of mum and dad, the first two were through.

Less self-conscious than her royal mother-in-law had been at the same age, Diana was never at a loss for something to say. 'I love playing bridge,' she told four old men when she walked in on their card school during a visit to the Nightingale Home for Elderly Jews. And when pensioner Marie Segal apologized for the fact that her hands were covered with flour—she was making apple strudel at the time—Diana insisted on shaking hands just the same. 'A little flour doesn't worry me,' she said. Commonplace as such remarks may sound, they are far from that to those to whom they are addressed. 'I will remember today for the rest of my life,' said a small spina bifida patient in Glasgow's Royal Hospital for Sick Children after the Princess had stopped to chat with her.

That particular visit to Glasgow started off ominously. A group calling itself the Scottish National Liberation Army sent a letter of protest to the Lord Provost, Dr Michael Kelly. To reinforce their protest, the senders of the letter enclosed a quantity of lighter fuel so that the letter was also a letter-bomb. Fortunately, the Lord Provost's secretary, Eric Hamilton, who opened the packet, escaped serious injury and was even able to join the party which welcomed the Princess. Told of the letter-bomb, she saw no reason why her programme should not go ahead as planned. That the so-called liberationists were hardly typical of the Scottish people was shown by the crowds who turned out to greet her as she picked her way through the mud and rubble of a housing estate to admire renovation work done by tenants. 'I'm dying for a cup of tea,' she told one couple as they showed her round their renovated flat. A pot of tea was quickly forthcoming. 'No milk or sugar, thank you,' said the figure-conscious Princess.

Invitations for her to go here, there and everywhere continued to stream in by every post. Of course, she could not possibly hope to accept them all, but she fitted in as many as possible, including one from Derek Attwell, headmaster of a school in Lee. It was the school's centenary year, he wrote, and they would love a visit from the Princess. So she visited the school, heard the children sing, unveiled a plaque to commemorate her visit and accepted a cuddly toy dog to take home for Prince William. The school-children were thrilled by it all; the Inner London Education Authority not so. They were 'shocked and horrified', they said, that the headmaster had presumed to

invite the Princess without reference to higher authority. Out
went a memorandum to all schools and colleges in the area that
any future invitations of that sort must be channelled through
ER/GP34 (which, for the benefit of the uninitiated, is the
External Relations and General Purposes Department). This
would then enable officials of the Authority to be present
on the occasion of any such visit, a spokesman explained.
One can well imagine with what bitter disappointment those
same officials faced the fact that, on this particular occasion,
they were simply closing the school gate after the Princess had
been and gone.

Some visits necessitated special precautions, though by now
the Princess was getting used to those. She wore a white overall
over her emerald green outfit, and a protective white hat, to tour
a pharmaceutical factory in Hertfordshire. Her husband was
similarly obliged to don a one-piece 'bunny suit' complete with
hood and outsize boots to tour a factory in Newport, one of three
he was shown round during a visit to that part of South Wales
nicknamed 'Silicon Valley' because of the micro-chips produced
there. 'I feel a right idiot,' he grumbled, good-naturedly.

It was around this time that the Prince disappeared
completely from the public scene for a few days. In an
atmosphere of cloak-and-dagger secrecy which Diana must
have wished could have applied to their skiing holiday, he spent
five days living and working on a farm on Dartmoor. If he had
not been born to be King, he would have loved to have been a
farmer, he has said, and this brief 'firsthand experience of what
life is like on a farm' was perhaps the next best thing. Daily from
seven in the morning until six at night or later, he worked
alongside Fred Hutchings and his son Wilfred on their 500-acre
farm, milking the cattle, muck-spreading the fields and, on one
occasion, helping to deliver a calf. Work done, he would slip
away each night to a private room in a nearby hotel from where
he called home to chat with Diana. He found the whole
experience 'most rewarding', he told her. Later he took her to
view the scene of his rural labours. They were on their way back
to Highgrove from a tour of Devon when he decided to divert
their helicopter so that she could have a look at the farm.

Whether or not his wife resented his hunting, as some gossip
columnists maintained, Charles continued to ride to hounds,
varying his hunting country both to confuse the Press and to

confound any anti-blood-sports demonstrators who might seek to make him the focus of protest.

It was while he was hunting with the Berkeley that his wife's fears for his safety were realized. His horse landed in a cart-track after taking a fence, stumbled, and the Prince was thrown. Fortunately, his injuries proved painful rather than serious, and he was able to remount after his horse had been caught and brought back, though a bruised face was in evidence that night when he and Diana attended a banquet at Caerphilly Castle. But it takes more than a few bruises to deter Prince Charles, and he was in the saddle again next day, this time with the Carmarthenshire Hunt.

It was time now to start preparing for their tours of Australia and New Zealand, postponed from the previous year because of Diana's pregnancy. For her, it would be the biggest test she had yet faced, six weeks of public exposure involving a travel schedule of some 45,000 miles. That travel itinerary could have been a few thousand miles less but for their wish to take William with them. Eager though they were to have him along, commonsense dictated that they could not simply pop him in his carry-cot and drag him around from place to place. For a baby of little more than nine months, which was all William would be at the time of the tour, that would be too much of a break with nursery routine. Instead, they arranged for what might be termed a 'home base' to be established in each country, Australia and New Zealand, where William could stay contentedly in the care of Nanny Barnes and with his parents flying back to visit him between their many public engagements. In Australia their choice was Woomargama, a homestead set amidst some four thousand acres of grazing land near Albury in New South Wales, with its millionaire owner Leonard Darling and his wife obligingly moving to their city home in Melbourne for the duration of the royal visit. Any reporter or photographer caught sneaking around the place would be deported, the Australian Government threatened.

Never before had a baby of so young an age been taken on a royal tour. As children, neither Charles nor Anne ever accompanied their parents. The nearest they came to it was when they sailed to Tobruk in the royal yacht *Britannia*, freshly commissioned at the time, to join the Queen and Prince Philip for the homeward leg of their 1953-4 Commonwealth tour.

Charles was five by then and Anne nearly four. The nearest any other member of the family has come to rivalling William in youthful travel was when the Duke of Gloucester was a baby. Towards the end of World War II he too journeyed to Australia with his parents. But that was not a royal tour. His father was going there for two years as Governor General.

The infant Prince Richard, as he was then, had made the long journey to Australia by sea. William and his parents would be going by air, no longer regarded, as it once was, as too hazardous for royal travel. True, the late Duke of Windsor, when he was a youthful Prince of Wales, insisted on piloting his own aircraft from place to place during a South American tour he undertook in the 1920s. Had he not abdicated the throne for love of Mrs Simpson, royal air travel might have become the vogue much sooner than it did. As it was, his successor, the Queen's father, resorted to flying only to visit the battlefronts of World War II, and it was left to Prince Philip, as a young naval officer who had always wanted to be a pilot, to make flying an accepted part of the royal way of life. Even so, the first major tour of the Queen's reign was still made by sea, though as a Princess she had already flown to Canada to deputize for her dying father. By now, it is estimated (though no one, unfortunately, has kept an exact record) that she has flown something like three-quarters of a million miles, and Prince Philip perhaps three times as much. Big though those figures are, they will probably seem small in the years to come, with young William's record for air travel far outstripping that of his grandparents.

As William's first overseas flight drew steadily nearer, only one problem remained to be resolved: Should father and baby son fly in the same aircraft? Flying separately would mean that either husband and wife were apart during the long flight to Australia (if Diana travelled with William) or that William would have to be content with his nanny for company. Neither alternative commended itself and the Queen herself saw no harm in Charles and William flying together while the second in line to the throne was still a baby, though when he was older, she thought, it would perhaps be wiser if they used separate aircraft.

When Diana had last flown to Australia, shortly after Prince Charles proposed to her, to get away from it all, and especially from the Press, she had been an ordinary bachelor girl whose clothes could be comfortably contained in no more than two suitcases. Luggage, this time, would run to something like ninety suitcases and trunks, though not all of them would be hers, of course. There would also be a few other items, such as William's baby-bouncer, which would not fit conveniently into any of the trunks or suitcases. On the occasion of that previous Australian trip she had been accompanied only by her mother and stepfather. This time she would be accompanied not only by her husband and baby son but, as Princess of Wales, by an entourage of a dozen or more, private secretaries and Press secretary, ladies-in-waiting and maids, valets and stenographers and security men. Also going along would be a physician, her personal hairdresser, Kevin Shanley, and of course William's nanny. Her husband's private secretary, Edward Adeane, and their Press secretary, Victor Chapman, had in fact already flown to Australia and New Zealand and back, checking on travel arrangements and timing, stopping off at the various places they would be visiting, to discuss their public engagements.

Prince Charles, of course, was already well versed in the *modus operandi* of the royal roadshow. For Diana, it would be a totally new experience, considerably longer in duration, far more extensive in its scope, busier, more rigorous and more exciting than the tour of Wales. Charles too was already knowledgeable about Australia, not only having been to school there but having returned for tours and flying visits more than half-a-dozen times since. He had toured New Zealand too and Tasmania, which they would also be visiting. Diana's first-hand knowledge of 'Down Under' was limited to the ten days of that pre-marriage holiday and to the beach area in New South Wales where she had stayed. There was much she did not know which she needed to know. So, with her husband as tutor, she settled down to do her homework.

10   Australia

The crowd in Brisbane that day, estimated later at more than a hundred thousand people, was the biggest the Princess had yet encountered (though there were even bigger crowds to come later). Vast and excited though the crowd was, she was quite composed as she embarked on the expected walkabout, smiling, pausing frequently to shake hands, accept flowers, say a few words. The din was almost incredible. 'Diana, Diana,' people shouted in unison, pressing forward more and more in their desire to see her, to touch her, to thrust flowers, gifts and Australian flags upon her. The sun blazed down hotly upon the incredible scene, pushing the temperature into the mid-eighties. The heat, the crowd and the excitement of Diana's presence combined to induce a sort of mass hysteria in those who pushed and struggled to see her. It was Charles, with his greater experience of crowd situations, who first sensed that this was like no reception they had previously experienced, and he tried to hurry her along. Diana herself seemed quite unaware of the effect she was creating and continued to take her time.

The chanting became louder, the pushing more frantic, the crowd a vast, seething mass in which people fainted and ribs were broken. Dozens had to be given on-the-spot first aid and three, two women and a child, taken to hospital. Those at the front began clambering over the barricades forming the walkabout route. A sudden surge of people separated the Princess from her husband. Unnerved, she looked round for him. Charles struggled his way back to her side. They were, just for a moment, in some danger of being bodily crushed by the press of people around them. Then their accompanying policemen cleared a space, linking arms to form a protective circle. With the Prince pulling and pushing his wife along, they managed to gain the safety of the town hall.

Breathless and shaken, the Princess sank gratefully into a convenient chair. Charles fetched her a cooling drink. The

Prince William travels the world: the family arrive at Alice Springs

Diana accepts a posy of flowers from a small girl at the Oval, Banbury in Western Australia

Prince Charles takes a fall during a polo game at Warwick Farm, near Sydney; but, a few days later, active as ever, he went swimming at Perth

Happy smiles sum up the bond between Charles and Diana

On board a massive Maori war canoe at Waitangi

The Princess exchanges a traditional greeting with a young Maori girl

Nanny Barnes carries eleven-month-old Prince William off the plane after his first royal tour

Watched by his wife and son, the heir to the throne plays with a toy plane during the photocall at Government House in Auckland

Sparkling at a state banquet in Halifax, Canada

The Princess of Wales with Canadian
Prime Minister Pierre Trudeau

At an 1890s costume banquet in
Edmonton. Diana's salmon-pink Thai
silk dress was worn by Francesca
Annis when she played Lillie Langtry,
mistress of Edward VII, in a TV series

The President of the Royal College of Music and his wife meet American singer Barry Manilow at his Festival Hall concert in aid of the RCM

Prince William at eighteen months with his mother in the grounds of Kensington Palace

Fashion note: Lady Diana Spencer at the age of nineteen, November 1980;
in stunning satin at the Barbican Centre; at the premiere of the James Bond
film *Octopussy*; dressed Cossack-style at the 1300th anniversary service at
Gloucester Cathedral

January 1984: Charles and Diana pose for a picture on the second day of their skiing holiday in Liechtenstein — thereafter the press and photographers generously left them alone

The Princess was already pregnant with her second child when she flew to Oslo in February 1984 to see the ballet *Carmen* performed by the London City Ballet of which she is patron

physician accompanying them was summoned to take a look at her. Outside the crowd continued its chant of 'Diana, Diana'. A brief rest of some ten minutes was sufficient to enable her to regain her composure, and she was smiling again when, to an explosion of cheers and whistles from the crowd, she appeared with her husband on the balcony of the town hall.

It was an experience of crowd hysteria sufficient to have unnerved anyone. 'Hellish' was the word used to describe it by one of the couple's Australian bodyguards. Yet at no other time, though they were involved in several situations almost as frenetic, did Diana show the slightest sign of wilting under the strains and stresses of what must surely have been the most frenetic royal tour ever. Despite the crowds, the frenzy, the heat, the extra travelling necessitated by the couple's desire to be with their baby son as much as possible, she stood up to it all like an experienced royal campaigner. 'The Princess is amazing,' said a member of their entourage at the midway stage of the tour. 'She just seems to go on and on.' Certainly the stamina she demonstrated belied all the earlier newspaper speculation about her health. Apart from that occasion in Brisbane, the services of the accompanying physician were required only once, and that was for a slight case of sunburn in the very early days of the tour.

In their six weeks in Australia and New Zealand, in addition to luncheons, banquets, balls and all manner of other official engagements, the royal couple took part in a hundred walk-abouts, changing clothes, because of the heat as well as the variety of engagements, several times a day. By the time it was all over, the Princess had been seen in something like fifty different outfits. And it was she, of course, whom everyone most wanted to see, with her husband content to bask in the reflected glory of her super-stardom. The jokes he had coined originally in Wales were trotted out again as the royal schedule went adrift day after day because of Diana's insistence on stopping to chat with people in the crowd. 'Sorry there's only one of her,' Charles apologized with mock solicitude. Mostly they appeared together on public occasions, though for each there was also the occasional solo engagement. In Adelaide, for instance, while Diana enjoyed a much-needed rest, Charles went on his own to watch a television film being shot. And in Fremantle, while Charles held an investiture, Diana opened a new hospital wing named after her.

The ever-growing crowds which flocked to see them as the tour progressed did little to help the republican aspirations of the recently elected Labour Government. While, admittedly, there were demonstrations here and there in favour of republicanism, loyalists clearly outnumbered would-be republicans by hundreds, perhaps thousands, to one. Those frenzied scenes in Brisbane, said the Queensland Premier. Johannes Bjelke-Petersen, provided 'conclusive evidence of the popularity of the Royal Family' and would make it harder for the Government to implement its republican ideas. 'It ought to make it clear to them,' he said, 'that they should leave questions like distancing themselves from the Royal Family and ignoring the traditions of the past well alone. We are fortunate, as a country, to have a Royal Family. Many other countries—the United States, for instance—would give almost anything to have something similar.' In any event, he added, if the Federal Government did try to push the country into republicanism, 'Queensland wouldn't be in it.'

Such views were echoed elsewhere. 'You may have heard doubts about republicanism,' the Tasmanian Premier, Robin Gray, told Prince Charles, 'but there are no such doubts here. We are one hundred per cent loyal to you and your family.' Even John Bannon, the Labour Premier of South Australia, did not seem to be entirely in favour of republicanism, speaking as he did of the monarchy's 'important constitutional role' and expressing the hope that the Prince and Princess would return many times to South Australia.

Prince Charles, in his public speeches, made no direct reference to the Labour Government's hope of phasing out the monarchy by the end of the century, with a president taking over. But he was perhaps referring to it obliquely in a speech he made in Melbourne when he spoke of the strong ties which bind Britain and Australia. 'These are ties,' he said, 'which do not diminish that strong sense of Australianism, of pride in a young country which is finding its own meaning and purpose in this part of the southern hemisphere.'

But if the Prince still nursed any faint hope that he might emulate his uncle, the late Duke of Gloucester, by becoming Governor General of Australia, such hope, despite the more than warm welcome he and Diana were accorded by the ordinary people of Australia, must have dissolved quickly under the impact of political reality. Since leaving the Navy, Charles has more and more felt the need for a real job of work, a role which would give him his own identity. Australia is a country with which he has forged ever stronger links since he was there as a schoolboy at the age of seventeen, and to have become Governor General would have been an ideal solution for him. Behind the scenes, the possibility has been discussed more than once. Malcolm Fraser, when he was Australia's prime minister, was said to have been in favour of the idea, but his political defeat shortly before the royal visit had put a very different complexion on things. The new Labour Prime Minister, Bob Hawke, while he was never less than completely courteous to the Prince and Princess, is pledged to republicanism, though his hopes of achieving that type of constitution, at least in the foreseeable future, clearly suffered a severe set-back as a result of the royal tour.

The tour started amidst the heat, dust and flies of Alice Springs, at the very centre of the vast land-mass of Australia. The flight had taken some thirty hours, with the clock going forward another nine because of the time difference. The Boeing 707 in which the couple made the trip had been specially adapted to provide a twin-bedded apartment for the royal parents and another for Nanny Barnes and baby William. The baby slept for much of the long flight. Diana slept less well. She and Charles were both 'very tired', she said on landing. The style of the tour was set immediately. Even the official welcome committee burst into spontaneous applause as the royal parents appeared at the top of the aircraft steps. There was another outburst of official cheers, and some less official shouts of 'Billy the Kid' from the crowd further off, as William was seen in the arms of his nanny. Diana took the baby from her, and Charles flicked away an inquisitive fly which sought to investigate the baby's face. 'His first fly,' said Charles, grinning. Having given the photographers the chance of some family pictures, Diana kissed William and passed him back to his nanny. Then some last-minute thought sent her dashing in pursuit as William was carried back into the aircraft for his onward flight to the 'nursery base' at Woomargama.

Recent events in the town called Alice saw the royal visitors having to make do with temporary accommodation. Three days of torrential rainfall had resulted in the worst floodwaters anyone in the area could remember, with the Alice Springs Casino, at which they were to have stayed, marooned and cut off. Arrangements were quickly put in hand to provide alternative accommodation at the Gap Motor Motel, with two adjoining suites being hurriedly converted, re-decorated and re-carpeted to provide a private dining-area and bar as well as sleeping-accommodation. The largest bed available had been manhandled into the bedroom, and there was already, in place of an ordinary bath, a wooden tub so massive that anyone taking a bath had to climb a couple of steps to get into it. The tub worked rather like 'a bubbling jacuzzi', the motel management explained. 'A love tub', the staff called it.

However, with the work of conversion not quite complete, a local car-dealer lent the royal couple his bungalow, furnished with reproduction antiques, for the first night of the tour. Diana was delighted to find that a swimming-pool went with the bungalow and promptly changed into a bikini to take a refreshing dip. Later, not yet sufficiently relaxed to face the crowd gathered outside the front of the motel, they dodged out through a gap in the rear fence to take a look at the flood damage.

If the style of the tour was to be spontaneous and demonstrative, the accent was to be on youth, and the following day found the couple at the Alice Springs School of the Air, sitting in front of microphones to answer questions from children living in the scattered homesteads of the sparsely populated 'Outback'. It was rather like *Mastermind*, Diana said as she settled herself at her microphone. As was only to be expected perhaps, many of the questions were about William. Did he have 'a bike' yet? Well, he was still a bit small for that, his mother replied. Did he have a favourite toy? A spot of diplomatic prompting from her husband resulted in Diana replying that he loved his toy koala bear. 'And he loves things that make noises,' she added. Another whispered prompt from Prince Charles. Oh, yes, and he had 'a little plastic whale which throws things out of the top—little balls'. What school would he go to? Charles himself decided to take over and answer this one. They would have to wait and see how his character developed. 'We might have to send him away to a school or two.' Could he crawl yet? 'No, not yet,' said Diana. 'He's got the right movement, but he hasn't done it yet. But he's got six teeth,' she added, proudly.

With questions coming over the air thick and fast, the occasion became more and more like an impromptu version of *Mastermind*. An eleven-year-old boy came up with a whole series of questions which very nearly stumped them. How big was Buckingham Palace? How many rooms did it have? 'I haven't a clue,' she confessed, neatly sidestepping the issue and passing it to her husband. 'You answer it.' Charles was similarly obliged to confess that he didn't know the number of rooms either, never having actually counted them. 'Even if I had, I daresay there would be quite a lot people didn't even know about. There might be someone who's been living there for years unbeknown to anyone.' Anyhow, he added, he and the Princess lived in Kensington Palace—'a smaller place'.

Later that day the couple flew to see the sun set over Ayers Rock, where they also had their first meeting with local Aborigines. There were more Aborigines next day at Tennant Creek, the town's normal 2,500 population having more than doubled in anticipation of the royal visit. Some had come in trucks from as far as 650 miles away. Already the couple were showing signs of over-exposure to the hot sun. Diana was ultra-pink in the face, while Charles' nose was peeling. It was perhaps inevitable that the Aborigines should present him with a boomerang. 'I should be able to get a pressman with this,' he quipped, slyly.

The country's newly elected Prime Minister, Bob Hawke, was on hand to greet them when they arrived in Canberra, the federal capital. Stolidly republican as he is, he did not bow to them. However, his wife Hazel dipped a curtsey, and his ageing father, who was also in the welcoming group, announced stoutly, 'I'm a Queen's man.' The Prime Minister entertained them to lunch, and they dined that night with Sir Ninian Stephen, the Governor General. For the people of Canberra, however, the highspot of the visit was the now almost obligatory walkabout. 'I wish I had a nanny like you to look after him,' said the mother of one small boy with whom the Princess stopped to talk. That the Princess was already missing her own small son was clear from her reply. 'I would swap with you any time,' she said. 'I wish I didn't have to leave William with a nanny.'

The saddest part of the tour was a visit to those areas of Victoria and South Australia which had been devastated by bush fires little more than a month before, a vista of blackened tree stumps and burnt-out homesteads. Forty-six people, twelve of them firemen, died in those terrible fires. They talked to the relatives of the dead, to the injured—some of them terribly injured—and to the homeless. 'My heart aches for you,' the Princess told the widow of one of the dead firefighters. 'We are so very sorry for you,' the Prince told another woman whose son had perished while trying to get through to the firefighters with refreshment.

It was perhaps inevitable that the tour, as it progressed, should sometimes become the focal point of protest. In Sydney a young man paraded with a green republican flag while his companion held up a placard bearing the words 'Go Home Royals.' An irate woman promptly grabbed the placard and ripped it in two. With an angry knot of loyalists surging round the flag-bearer, police moved in, as much to protect the protesters as anything else. Ten thousand young people packed the area in front of the Sydney Opera House to hear a speech by Prince Charles which touched exactly the right chords. He had first set foot in Australia, he recalled, as a teenaged schoolboy, 'a hesitant Pom in this vast and exciting land'. But he had been made to feel 'utterly at home', and returning now was like bringing his wife and son to meet old friends. He was pleased, he said, that a small portion of his baby son's 'impressionable subconscious will be filled with the sounds and scents of the great Australian outdoors. In the days to come I hope he will grow to regard this country with affection and admiration as she develops into a future of considerable promise.' How well the Princess had done her homework prior to the tour was revealed when it came to the singing of 'Advance Australia Fair'. She had been given a songsheet but left it on her chair as she stood to join in the singing. She knew the words off by heart.

In his speeches, Charles referred frequently to his wife and son. Sometimes seriously; sometimes jokingly. Joking comes naturally to him. During his spell as a schoolboy in Australia, one of his stock jokes was that among the things he was being taught at Timbertop was how to catch kangaroos. You crept up on them from behind, caught them by the tail and flipped them over onto their backs. He told it so well that some people believed him. Some people believed him too when, in the course of one luncheon speech he made during the royal tour, he joked that he and Diana were raising William on a diet of warm milk and minced kangaroo meat. 'No doubt he will turn into a huge, healthy *and bouncing* boy,' he quipped. Back in Britain, when reports of the speech had appeared in the newspapers, Buckingham Palace found itself inundated with protests that kangaroo meat was not suitable for such a young baby. 'It was meant to be a joke,' Charles explained when he heard what was happening back home, and promptly went on to make another. 'In fact, we are bringing him up on grass and beer.'

It was that teenage spell of schooling in Australia, Charles always says, which first brought him out of his 'shell'. In consequence, he always seems to be at his most uninhibited when in Australia. Perhaps the less deferential Australian attitude to royalty bounces back off him. Certainly a charity ball in Sydney, where he and Diana led off the dancing, found him in exuberant mood. With the band playing 'The More I See You', they started in dignified, almost hesitant, fashion. However, Charles stepped up the pace to a quickstep which he then quickened still more until the two of them were jiving, whirling round almost dizzily, while the rest of the guests applauded enthusiastically.

Although they stayed late at the ball, Charles was up early the following morning, cresting the waves at Bondi Beach. If most of the people who thronged to watch royal walkabouts had eyes mainly for Diana, there was still a small feminine contingent with a more than passing interest in her husband. Two of them—topless—were at Bondi Beach that morning, and it took the combined efforts of local police, Charles' own security men, a royal equerry and the physician accompanying the royal party to ensure that they did not get close enough to make the Prince's acquaintance. Diana too went swimming that day, though in rather less robust fashion. She does not particularly care for swimming in the sea—she does not like the waves, she says—and contented herself with a few lengths of the pool at Government House. And back at the nursery base at Woomargama, baby William was swimming too. At least, with his nanny holding him securely and a pair of water-wings for additional support, he splashed about in the pool there. 'He loved it and was not a bit afraid of the water,' revealed one of the royal staff.

'I miss him, but he doesn't miss me,' the Princess told people in Tasmania who asked about the baby. However, the tour schedule had been arranged so that she and Charles could fly to

Woomargama to be with William every few days. They were
with him most weekends as well as over Easter and were
delighted, on one visit, to find that he had another tooth coming
through, his seventh. Like themselves, he was also, they
saw, becoming healthily tanned. Diana, on these visits to
Woomargama, would herself take William for his dip in the
pool, and one day, with Charles away playing polo, she also took
the baby with her in a Range Rover to explore Woomargama's
4,000 acres. She had hoped to show him a kangaroo, she said on
her return, but they hadn't seen any.

Good and bad news from home reached her while she was in
Australia. The good news was that her sister Jane, wife of the
Queen's assistant private secretary, had produced a baby
brother for her three-year-old daughter. The bad news was that
Diana's seventy-four-year-old grandmother, Ruth, Lady Fermoy,
lady-in-waiting to the Queen Mother, had returned to her
Eaton Square flat one night just too late to prevent thieves
making off with her jewellery.

With each fresh walkabout the crowds became bigger and
more frenetic. What happened in Maitland, New South Wales,
served as a warning as to what might happen in the future—and
what very nearly did happen in Brisbane. In Maitland, where
the crowd was much smaller, people still surged past the
barriers, pushed policemen and pressmen out of the way and all
but mobbed the royal couple. 'It was more like Beatlemania
than a royal tour,' said a police officer. So hysterical did the
crowd become that people fainted and others were knocked
down, children cried and women screamed, and more than a
hundred people had to be given some form of first aid. To enable
Charles and Diana to get through to the civic centre, the police
had to form themselves into a human wedge around and ahead
of them. The lesson did not go unheeded, and civic authorities in
towns and cities yet to be visited by the royal couple were
warned what to expect. Tasmania, next stopping-place on the
tour schedule, promptly increased its police requirement for the
royal visit by some twenty-five per cent.

Controversy over the Franklin hydro-electric dam was at its
height when the couple arrived in Tasmania. Wisely, Prince
Charles steered clear of the subject in the speech he made at a
state reception. For the most part his speech was in lighthearted
vein with the now customary references to his wife and son. He

recalled that when he was last in Tasmania he had received many congratulatory messages on his engagement to 'a lovely lady'. He added, to applause, 'As you can see, I was lucky enough to marry her.' Such public praise from her husband seemed to embarrass the Princess. She blushed and screwed her face into a mock grimace. Charles saw her. 'It's amazing what ladies will do when your back is turned,' he joked. There were other jokes too: the one about raising William on a diet of grass and beer, and another about Australia's wedding gift having ensured that William was born 'with at least six silver spoons in his mouth'. For his wife, he said, their Australian visit was 'something of a crash course', and he went on to add a sentence or two which were perhaps not entirely without political significance in view of the Labour Government's known objection to future royal tours, expressing the hope that there would be 'many other occasions when I can visit Tasmania. There are so many other places I would like to take my wife to and so many other people I would like to introduce her to.'

A polo game at Warwick Farm, near Sydney, was also the occasion of an unexpected reunion for the Princess. She had gone there with Charles to watch him take part in an exhibition game. Waiting to meet her, to her surprise and delight, was Anne Bolton, one of the three girls who had shared her London flat in pre-marriage days. In Australia on a working holiday, she had journeyed from Queensland specially to meet the Princess. 'I don't believe it,' Diana gasped as they ran to greet each other. Though it was not the first time they had met since the royal wedding—they had both been guests at Carolyn Pitman's wedding since—it was the first opportunity they had had to exchange notes, so anxious had Diana been to get back to William on the occasion of their previous meeting. But if William took priority, polo did not, and Diana became so engrossed in all Anne had to say, and all she had to tell Anne, that she saw little of the game. For the record, the President's team, for which Charles was playing, won 9-6.

And she saw nothing at all of a subsequent game in which her husband fell from, slipped from or was knocked off his polo pony. While that was going on, Diana was at Woomargama with William. Charles himself claims he was knocked off—'with the accent on "knocked" for all those who think I just fall off all the time'. But the opponent with whom he had this close encounter, Richard Walker, said afterwards, 'Falling is just part of the game.' As those who saw the incident on television will know, Charles appeared to over-reach himself in an attempt to hit the ball and then slip from the saddle in an elegant, slow-motion fashion which gave the ever-watchful photographers sufficient time to take a whole series of shots recording this particular royal fall from grace.

So far, demonstrations pro-this or anti-that had been either so small or so far removed from where the royal couple actually were as to be almost unnoticed by them. In Adelaide, however, they became the focal point of several vociferous minority groups. Pro-republican flags, 'Free Ireland' placards and chants of 'British murderers' greeted them as they drove up to the town hall. Later that day, protesters picketed Government House while the royal couple were dining there. As on other occasions, the small number of demonstrators was vastly outnumbered by the thousands of loyal Australians who lined the streets in welcome.

Each fresh stopping-place had its quota of unrehearsed, unexpected incidents. For Prince Charles, in Port Pirie, there was a briefly embarrassing reminder of his bachelor days when it was kisses all the way. 'I do hope Lady Diana will not mind if I give you a kiss,' said the sixteen-year-old captain of St Mark's School, Rebecca La Forgia, as the Prince presented her with a prize on sports day. Charles blushed, looked hesitantly at Diana and queried 'Well?' Looking equally embarrassed, Diana could hardly say anything but 'Go on then.' Rebecca got not only her kiss but a handshake from the Princess. 'You're so beautiful,' she told Diana.

In Perth it was Diana's turn to be kissed. And if Rebecca had at least had the courtesy to ask before kissing Prince Charles, twelve-year-old Michael Edmiston saw no need for such formality. As Diana took his outstretched hand, he simply held on, pulling her forward until she almost over-balanced and then planting a kiss on her cheek. 'I'd been planning to do that all along,' he said with a deal of boyish satisfaction.

Things also went briefly, if amusingly, wrong in Bunbury where the Prince was due to address a rally of some three thousand schoolchildren. Quoting from the advice set down by an Australian mother towards the end of the previous century, he proceeded to caution his youthful audience against aggression and falsehood, against being revengeful or ill-tempered. At that point in his homily a sudden gust of wind blew away a page of his notes. 'God, my bloody bit of paper,' he muttered in a voice loud enough for the microphone to pick up and transmit. If that was not bad enough, worse was to follow. The errant paper was retrieved and passed back to him and he continued with his speech, only to find that the next bit of nineteenth-century advice he was required to pass on consisted of the admonition, 'Swearing is contemptible and foolish.'

Earlier that day he had again taken advantage of the nearness of the sea to enjoy an early-morning dip in the surf. Members of his entourage closed protectively around him as they spotted a sun-tanned beauty in a striped swimsuit cleaving the water in his direction. It had all the signs of developing into the sort of situation royal security men find most difficult to handle. Fortunately, the situation resolved itself. 'Hello, Lesley,' said Charles. 'Hello, Charles,' said Lesley Meadmore, who had first met the Prince when he was previously in Australia some four years earlier. They caught up on each other's news as they swam together, Lesley telling Charles about her two small children, and him telling her about William. 'He's just starting to crawl,' said the proud royal father. 'Just wait until he starts to walk,' warned the young Australian mother.

If an estimated one hundred thousand people packed the city centre of Brisbane when the royal couple went there, there was to be twice that number in Melbourne, with the entire city centre brought to a standstill. However, police reinforcements wisely brought in just ahead of the couple's arrival ensured that there was no repetition of the mob scenes which had erupted at Brisbane and elsewhere. The customary walkabout passed off smoothly and without incident, with the Princess moving deftly from one side of the route to the other in an attempt to come as near as possible to splitting herself in halves. As always, she was inundated with flowers and gifts for the baby. Already she had been given more than sufficient gifts for perhaps half-a-hundred babies and, as in Britain, she and Charles arranged for the bulk of them to be passed on to children's homes and orphanages.

The Australian section of their 'Down Under' tour ended with a farewell ball at the Melbourne Hilton. If Diana's daytime outfits, for reasons explained earlier, had sometimes attracted a degree of criticism, there was nothing but admiration for the dress she wore that night, a show-stopping, figure-hugging creation in white silk crêpe sparkling with crystal embroidery. 'Sensational' was perhaps the only word adequately to describe it—and it was a word used time and again by others at the ball, by critics and commentators and by those who saw the Princess that night on television.

11   New Zealand

The Australian section of the royal tour 'Down Under' had lasted just three days short of a month, during which time the Prince and Princess had visited all parts of that vast sub-continent. Now, with William and their back-up group of ladies-in-waiting, maids, valet, hairdresser, physician, secretaries and security men, they flew on to New Zealand, to Auckland, where William was settled in a room at Government House just across from the suite occupied by his parents.

Though the youngest of her own children was now ten and out of the nursery stage, Lady Beattie, the wife of the Governor General, Sir David Beattie, had been at some pains to ensure that William had a proper nursery for the period of his parents' visit. To this end, she had decorated his room with mobiles she had designed herself, installed a screen adorned with animal pictures and provided a selection of suitable toys. There was even a new quilt for the cot the royal parents had brought with them from home, some of the *appliqué* work on which Lady Beattie had also done herself. And with the baby Prince now at the crawling stage, she had had a swing gate installed at the head of the stairs as a safeguard against possible tumbles. If William himself was still too young in years to appreciate all that had been done on his behalf, his parents were delighted—as they were with the scatter cushions in antique lace which their hostess had made for their own suite. To top it all, Lady Beattie produced for William's use the pram she had kept carefully stored away since her own children outgrew it. She had had a new canopy fitted to replace the one gnawed by the dog, she explained.

The Prince and Princess were greeted on their arrival in Auckland by rain (which was to continue to fall throughout much of their visit), by the Prime Minister, Robert Muldoon, and by the shouted slogans of a group protesting over the question of Maori rights. However, they avoided a demonstration planned by some IRA supporters. That particular bunch of demonstrators somehow found themselves at the wrong terminal when the royal aircraft touched down.

There was, as the royal couple quickly saw, considerable discontent among New Zealand's Maori population at that time. But if some Maoris made the visit the occasion for protest, others were concerned to welcome them warmly and loyally. There was the traditional nose-rubbing greeting for the Princess when she and Charles arrived at a sports stadium in Auckland where some 35,000 youngsters had gathered to see them. For her husband, there was the equally traditional Maori challenge, the first of several he was to find himself facing during the course of their stay in New Zealand. This initial challenge was posed by a group of schoolboys dressed for the occasion in reed skirts, their faces fearsomely painted. The leading 'warrior' of the group grimaced at the royal visitors, poked out his tongue, uttered menacing cries and made threatening gestures with a spear. Make-believe though it all was, the Princess was fascinated. Prince Charles, of course, had seen it all before on previous visits to New Zealand and knew what was expected of him. When a ceremonial stick was thrown to the ground in front of him, he accepted the 'challenge' by picking it up and all was well.

The weather was fine enough that day for them to move freely from group to group, the Prince beaming with pleasure as he watched the accomplished way in which his wife now handled everything. The following day, however, when they visited a boating centre on Auckland's north shore, saw the return of the rain. The brass band tried to make light of it by playing 'Raindrops', but the royal couple were obliged to borrow raincoats and umbrellas to walk round a playing-field which the incessant rain soon turned into a quagmire. To add to their troubles, more water was splashed over them by children demonstrating water-rescue techniques in one of the pools, and the Princess nearly lost a shoe as one heel sank too deeply into the muddy surface of the playing-field. A length of red carpet was quickly produced and unfurled for her to walk on, but this too was soon soaked with rain and streaked with mud. To top it all, the royal Rolls selected that particular day to stage a breakdown, and they had to wait a further ten minutes before a replacement Daimler arrived to convey them back to the dryness and comfort of Government House.

This New Zealand part of the couple's 'Down Under' trip continued to experience a few hiccups. If it wasn't rain, it was protesters, it seemed. At Wellington, during a walkabout in the city centre, there was some degree of jeering and cat-calling. The Prince, of course, had experienced this sort of thing before, as far back as those days in Wales which led up to his installation as Prince of Wales, but it is never pleasant. To the Princess, it was still a new experience. However, she carried on walking, talking, smiling and shaking hands, maintaining an appearance of being calm and unruffled, as loyalists in the crowd took matters into their own hands and the police were obliged to move in and intervene in the scuffling. There had been a protest of a different sort as the couple drove from the airport earlier that day. A Maori stepped forward from the crowd as their car drew level, turned his back, bent over and flipped up his reed skirt to bare his buttocks. Despite his contention that buttock-bearing was a traditional Maori protest, he was later fined the New Zealand equivalent of £185 for offensive behaviour.

At a banquet that evening Prince Charles took the opportunity publicly to thank New Zealand for the loyal way it had rallied to Britain's support at the time of the Argentine invasion of the Falkland Islands. Recalling how promptly the country had severed diplomatic relations with Argentina and how quickly it had dispatched a frigate to the Indian Ocean in order to free a British frigate for the fighting in the South Atlantic, the Prince said: 'The fact that you decided to send help in such a hurry was much appreciated.' He could be assured of New Zealand's overwhelming loyalty to the Crown, the Prime Minister told him.

Almost as though the Maori protesters had cast a spell over the royal tour, things continued to go wrong. In Wainuiomata, Press photographers from Britain staged a lightning strike and downed cameras. New Zealand photographers were being favoured with all the best photographic positions, they maintained. However, a meeting later in the day between royal aides and photographers saw things settled amicably. Then a ball at Government House, coinciding with the Queen's fifty-seventh birthday, got off to an embarrassing start when some six hundred guests found themselves squeezing into a ballroom which would normally hold only half that number in comfort. Diana looked radiant in a gown of apricot taffeta and a pearl-

and-diamond tiara given to her by the Queen. Known in the
Royal Family as 'Granny's tiara', it was in fact one which the
Queen herself had been given by her grandmother, Queen
Mary. The royal couple stood with the Governor General and
Lady Beattie on a dais at one end of the ballroom. The Governor
General asked the guests to top up their glasses in readiness to
toast the Queen on her birthday. Guests looked at each other in
consternation. What glasses? There were none. And even if
there had been, there was nothing with which to top them up.
Goblets and champagne were quickly rustled up for those on the
dais if not for everyone else, and Sir David proposed the toast.
The royal couple drank from their glasses. From the look on the
Prince's face, it was not champagne but something rather
inferior. He reached over to take his wife's glass from her hand
and set both glasses quickly to one side.

With so much going wrong, however trivial, in so many
different directions, it needed some sort of royal set-piece to get
the show back on the road. Charles and Diana produced just
that—with a little help from William. A rug was spread in the
grounds of Government House, and from it the baby Prince,
now ten months old, held his first Press conference, attended by
some thirty reporters and almost twice as many photographers.
If William was not yet of an age to answer questions, he did
manage one small comment which the assembled reporters
interpreted as 'Dada'. But maybe it was 'Papa', that being the
style of address between son and father more common in royal
circles. If the reporters got little out of the occasion, the
photographers had a field day, clicking their cameras non-stop
as William demonstrated his ability to crawl. An attempt to
crawl right off the rug and investigate the grass beyond was
checked by his father who, notwithstanding the Buckingham
Palace edict that William's name should not be abbreviated,
was heard to call his son 'Wills'. The proud father did his best to
make up for his son's inability to answer questions. 'He wants to
stand up all the time now,' he told the assembled pressmen.
With some help from his parents, William demonstrated again,
not only standing up but taking a few toddling steps between
mum and dad. And while he himself had not yet faced up to the
traditional Maori challenge, he showed his ability to deliver it,
sticking out his tongue at the reporters and photographers.
'Who's a little superstar, then?' inquired his mother.

If Charles could call the baby 'Wills', the ordinary New Zealander saw no reason why he should not equally be called 'Willy'. 'How is Willy?' the Prince found himself being asked in the course of a subsequent walkabout. 'In wonderful condition,' he replied. 'Very dangerous—he knocks everything about.'

The Prince's brother Edward was also in New Zealand at this time, in accordance with the policy that the Queen's sons should obtain part of their education in a Commonwealth country. Charles himself had been to school in Australia, Andrew in Canada; for Edward it was New Zealand, though as a junior master rather than a schoolboy at Wanganui College. He had been unable to meet his brother and sister-in-law on their arrival at Auckland, having flown to Australia two days earlier to spend a few days with one of his old tutors from Gordonstoun. Nor was he able to attend the ball at Government House, though he had been invited. He had to rehearse for a school play, he explained. All three finally got together at the college, where Edward, having been made an honorary Maori chieftain during his stay in New Zealand (as Andrew had earlier been made an honorary Indian chief in Canada), turned out to greet his big brother in a Maori ceremonial cloak of many feathers. 'What the hell is that you're wearing?' Charles asked, teasingly. Edward, for his part, was embarrassed by the presence of photographers and a television crew. The shyest of the Queen's sons, a young Prince who prefers to maintain a low profile, he did his best to keep his feathered back to the cameras.

Charles and Diana were themselves to play the leading parts in more than one Maori ceremony during those two weeks in New Zealand. There was a full ceremonial welcome for them at the Maoris' sacred meeting-place near Gisborne, not far from the spot where Captain Cook first landed in New Zealand over two centuries before. Beside this, the schoolboy welcome they had been accorded in Auckland seemed but a pale imitation. This was the real thing, or nearly so, full-blooded to the extent that the Princess looked a shade apprehensive as the leading 'warrior' pranced and gesticulated menacingly in front of her and her husband. Someone should have told her that in everyday life, minus his war-paint, the 'warrior' was a solicitor in Auckland. Charles, however, handled the challenge as confidently as he had dealt with the schoolboy one in Auckland, and Maori 'threats' gave way to songs and dances of welcome as well as a considerable amount of nose-rubbing all round. Sir Henare-Ngata, chairman of the Tairawhiti Maori Council, in his speech of welcome to the couple, referred only obliquely to the Maoris' grievances over the land lost to them by the 1840 Treaty of Waitangi, saying that, while the treaty was good as a whole, it left much to be desired. Charles, in his reply, delighted his Maori hosts by addressing them in their own tongue. If there were a few titters among his listeners at his pronunciation here and there, there were also loud cheers for a brave effort. It had been the best day of their visit to New Zealand, Charles said as they left.

Rain returned to mar proceedings when the royal couple attended a commemorative service at the Anzac Day Memorial in Auckland. It came in a sudden downpour right in the middle of the ceremony. An umbrella was eventually found for the Princess, but by that time she was already wet. As for Charles, with no umbrella to protect him as he stood nearest the memorial on his own, he was thoroughly soaked. There was a further downpour on the day they visited Dunedin. Nevertheless, with Charles holding an umbrella over his wife, they continued their walkabout, shaking wet hands and accepting dripping bouquets.

It had been anticipated that any serious demonstration by Maori protesters would come on the day the couple visited Waitangi, where the controversial treaty had been signed nearly a century and a half earlier. So tight security was in force when they went there. In the event, things passed off quietly from the security viewpoint if not entirely smoothly in other ways. It had been arranged that they should approach the ancient treaty ground by sea. To this end, a massive war canoe, built from two mighty tree trunks and nearly 120 feet long, awaited them. The Princess as well as the Prince was to travel by war canoe, the first woman to be accorded that privilege. Not even the Queen had been granted it on previous visits to New Zealand, and it was perhaps as well that she had not, as things turned out.

The royal couple were handed aboard and took their places in the middle of the canoe. The paddlers were all set to paddle. Unfortunately, the mighty canoe had been left high and dry by the receding tide and first had to be cumbersomely manhandled into the water. Once afloat, the paddlers experienced considerable difficulty in manoeuvring it because of its great length.

Worse still, it was found to be leaking, with the honoured visitors in danger of getting their feet wet. However, they finally made it to the treaty ground without actually capsizing—and even that seemed a possibility at one point—to be greeted by songs of welcome. The only protest of the day came that evening when an egg splattered on the windscreen of their car as they drove to a farewell banquet in Auckland.

The banquet found Charles in customary jocular vein. 'I have come to the conclusion,' he said in his farewell speech, 'that it really would have been easier to have had two wives. Then they could cover both sides of the street and I could have walked down the middle directing operations.' However, the one wife he did have, he added, had proved herself 'as good as any woman at the art of hong-ing', which is the Maori custom of rubbing noses. Becoming more serious, he expressed the hope that bringing their baby with them had helped 'to revive that family feeling which my wife and I think is so important'.

Then it was all over, six strenuous weeks in which the two of them had covered a total of some 45,000 miles and experienced hot sun and torrential rain in the course of a hundred walkabouts during which they had shaken hundreds of hands and been seen by thousands. Charles, of course, had been through it all before, many times. For Diana, it had all been new and exciting if also gruelling. Only once had she wilted, and then only briefly. For the rest, she had carried things off with charm and style and warmth, the new superstar of the royal family. Now it was time for a thoroughly deserved rest.

From New Zealand they flew first to Los Angeles, where they kissed baby William goodbye. He was flying back to Britain with Nanny Barnes and the rest of the royal entourage. His parents boarded a private jet made available to them on loan and flew to Eleuthera in the Bahamas for a short, away-from-it-all holiday with Lord and Lady Romsey, to whose baby daughter Diana is godparent as Lord Romsey is to Prince William. Their previous holiday with the same couple on the same island, when Diana was pregnant with William, had been partly spoilt for them by the presence of photographers; this time they hoped that their wish 'for an entirely private holiday will be respected'. After the furore which had erupted on the previous occasion, Britain's newspapers, at least, were ready to oblige.

12 Canada

Photographers' cameras clicked away more industriously than ever, and people too polite actually to stare darted surreptitious glances in Diana's direction when she arrived at Smith's Lawn, Windsor, on the last Sunday of May 1983, to watch her husband play polo. The cause of the even-busier-than-usual photographers and the more-than-slightly-interested glances was a remark Charles himself had made some three days before, when he opened a new extension to the London Business School. At the luncheon which followed the opening ceremony, Sir Terence Beckett joked that the royal baby, Prince William, would probably be a grown man before the school could afford another extension. It was in response to this that Charles made the remark which set people speculating whether his wife was again pregnant.

'I would only like to say,' he said, 'that the breeding programme is now firmly under way to make sure that there are future exponents of the art of opening extensions.'

Speculation that the Princess might be expecting another baby was bolstered by the fact that the royal couple, in the wake of their long tour of Australia and New Zealand, had not long returned from a relaxing ten-day holiday on the island of Eleuthera. What better time or place for a busy Princess to conceive? But like the reference to the minced kangaroo meat on which he had told Australians Prince William was being fed, the remark was just another of Charles' little jokes, it seemed. 'You cannot make a joke anywhere,' he commented, ruefully, when he realized what the result of his remark had been, while his Press secretary gave a firm 'No' to newspaper inquiries. 'The Princess has put on a little weight, but she is definitely not pregnant.'

The newspapers, however, having been tossed another angle to the non-stop story of the Superstar Princess, were naturally reluctant to relinquish it. Photographs were published of the slightly plumper Diana who had returned from Eleuthera in such a way as to suggest that plumpness was indeed pregnancy. Captions were devised to suggest that her fresh bloom of beauty was due to something more than a mere ten-day holiday. Possible conception was even antedated to before the holiday in order that the possibility of a Christmas baby could be mooted. A remark by the Prince's personal detective, Inspector Colin Trimming, did not help to quell the rumours. Asked on another occasion why the Princess was not at Windsor to watch Charles play polo, he was quoted as saying, 'This morning sickness does terrible things, you know.' Another joke? Hindsight answers, 'Obviously.' But, at the time, Press secretary Victor Chapman was obliged to issue another statement which, if not an exact denial, was the next best thing: 'If and when she does become pregnant, the Princess will announce it in her own good time.'

The Prince's own subsequent behaviour was hardly designed to make life easier for the newspapers or for his own Press officer, who had to deal with the continuing inquiries. Attending a reception arranged by the Royal College of Arms, he mused aloud on whether he had been invited because of a 'generations-long, rather uncontrolled experiment in breeding'. Indeed, as though deliberately teasing the newspapers, he used the word 'breeding' no fewer than three times. 'He does go on about it,' Diana sighed. Inadvertently perhaps, she herself was responsible for stimulating public curiosity further. Opening the Royal Preston Hospital in Lancashire, she chanced to ask if there had been an outbreak of the current German measles epidemic in the area. Her question about a disease with particular relevance to unborn children was immediately seized upon by some newspapers as another pointer to possible pregnancy.

In fact, Diana's healthy and slightly plumper appearance was due to nothing more than the relaxing holiday and good meals she and Charles had enjoyed on Eleuthera. Those ten days of resting, eating, paddling, swimming and sunbathing, with no crowds mobbing them and no pressmen dogging their heels, acted as a complete antidote to their six hectic weeks in Australia and New Zealand. They returned to Britain, with an extra layer of sun-tan and Diana's hair bleached a shade or two lighter still, on a scheduled British Airways flight from Miami. But not as ordinary passengers. The upstairs lounge of the aircraft afforded special privacy. In place of the customary airline food, they were served such delicacies as lobster canapés, caviar, smoked duckling, trout and noisette of lamb, while the scheduled in-flight movie was replaced, for their special benefit, by a showing of *Sting II*, a film which had not then been released in Britain.

Jet-lag has little or no effect on Prince Charles. Despite that overnight flight from Miami, he was out and about on royal duty that same evening, attending a dinner given by the Worshipful Company of Fishmongers. Diana too, after a day spent reunited with baby William, was busy the following day, visiting handicapped children in the vicinity of her Gloucestershire home. By then Charles was on his way north to Scotland for the dedication ceremony of a new North Sea oil-production platform.

The Princess, her list of appointments continuing to grow steadily if gradually, added the Red Cross Youth and Junior Volunteers to her other patronages and presidencies. More and more she was confident and experienced enough now to undertake public engagements without the support of her husband. With Charles in Oxford receiving a diploma in civil law, she journeyed to Newcastle on Tyne to open a new bridge. While there, she also donned white overalls and hat to look round a new food factory. She found pizzas 'so good for popping under a hot grill', she revealed, surprisingly. And while Charles was attending the annual meeting of the Royal Naval Film Corporation, she was in Canterbury, visiting an old people's centre. She was amused and delighted to be given an outsize teddy bear. 'Is it for Prince Charles or my baby?' she asked, laughing.

Delighting in each other's company as they do, there were also many functions the couple elected to attend together. They went together to a Renaissance exhibition at Sutton Place, home of the late Paul Getty. They were together at a concert at the Albert Hall to celebrate the centenary of the Royal College of Music's gaining its royal charter. They were together at the Dorchester for a luncheon in aid of the Injured Jockeys' Fund and the Leukaemia Research Fund. Prince Charles, on that occasion, presented an award to Ben de Haan for the year's most outstanding feat of horsemanship (his Grand National victory on 'Corbière'). There was also a trip to Bodmin together to visit Duchy of Cornwall properties in the area, and it was during a walkabout in St Columb Major that a young man, following the example of the precocious twelve-year-old in Australia, kissed the Princess on the cheek. 'You are supposed to shake hands,' she reprimanded him, blushing prettily.

The Muldoons, who had entertained them so hospitably in New Zealand, were now in London, and they entertained them in return at Kensington Palace. The Sultan of Brunei was another visitor. With a General Election now in the offing, Prince Charles had a small bet on the outcome with Michael Foot, then leader of the Labour Party. It would be a 'hung Parliament', the Prince wagered. However, the Tories' landslide victory was to prove him wrong, and he paid up with a vintage bottle of claret. Busy as he was in so many different directions around this time, Charles also managed to sandwich in a number of polo games. Sometimes Diana would go along to watch; sometimes not. Newspaper reports that polo did not interest her were denied by her husband's polo manager, Ronnie Ferguson. 'The Princess is not a horsewoman herself, but she does enjoy watching her husband play,' he insisted.

At home, Prince William was not only growing all the time but becoming steadily more agile and venturesome. To the delight and amusement of his parents, he could now manage to toddle round a room on his own, using items of furniture for support as he went. They both thought him 'a very energetic little chap'. They discussed whether or not they should take 'Wills' with them on their forthcoming tour of Canada. The people of Canada, they knew, would be delighted to feel that the baby was on Canadian soil even if they never actually got to see him. Of more personal concern to the royal parents was the fact that, if they did not take him, they would be apart from him on his first birthday. Against the idea of taking William with them was the fact that the tour would be a much shorter one than that from which they had so recently returned, only two weeks as against the six weeks they had spent in Australia and New Zealand. The shorter time inevitably meant a more crowded itinerary and fewer opportunities to be with William between engagements. There was also the question of where to leave him if they took him with them. They would be using the royal yacht *Britannia* as a base for much of the trip, and to have William on board might result in his suffering from sea-sickness. All things considered, they eventually decided, however reluctantly, that it might be best if he remained at home. It was unfortunate that that would also mean missing his birthday, but their feeling was that he was 'too young to notice', it was stated on their behalf.

That decision taken, they settled to do their 'homework'. Charles' researches led him to the discovery that he would be the fourth Prince of Wales to visit Nova Scotia, which was to form part of their itinerary. Charles also found a note in the royal archives which his great-grandfather, later King George V, had made after going there in 1901. He had counted the amount of hand-shaking he was required to do and ended with the staggering total of 24,855 hands shaken.

The six weeks the Prince and Princess were to spend in Canada served to discount all theories of possible pregnancy. Royalty-watchers with memories long enough to recall another royal tour of Canada nearly a quarter of a century before were able to compare the Princess's reactions in 1983 with those of her mother-in-law in 1959. Despite all denials, the Queen was unquestionably pregnant with Prince Andrew when she toured Canada on that occasion. There were times when she looked tired and strained, one day at least when she was forced to cancel her engagements and stay in bed, and there was an occasional degree of tetchiness on the part of Prince Philip. With Charles and Diana, in 1983, there was a complete absence of similar telltale signs, though Charles continued to tease Press and public, and sometimes embarrass his wife, by making frequent references to the possibility of further children.

In Nova Scotia he spoke of bringing 'our children' to Canada with them on future visits. 'There may be several of them by then,' he said, 'though that is not a hint, I assure you.' This with a sideways glance at his wife, who blushed. He was at it again in Newfoundland. 'As parents,' he said, 'we realize the responsibility we have to our one child, and I hope to have several more in the future.' Again he darted a teasing glance at his wife, and again she blushed. It seemed to be a subject very much on his mind. 'This could lead to a baby boom,' he joked in Ottawa when their tour schedule was interrupted by an unexpected power cut.

Royal tours are timed to the minute and normally run like clockwork. But in Canada, as in Australia and New Zealand, the new-style informality which the couple have brought to the royal public appearances, their inclination to pause and chat with those met along the way, necessitated frequent last-minute adjustments to their time-schedule. On arrival, for instance, instead of leaving directly from the Shearwater air base in Nova Scotia where their Canadian Boeing 707 touched down, they paused to chat with Canadian servicemen and their families. An hour later found them at the Garrison Grounds in the centre of Halifax, where some six thousand square feet of new turf had been specially laid for them to walk on. There was the inevitable chorus of 'We want Di', this time with a Canadian accent, as the Princess appeared in an outfit echoing the red and white of Canada's national colours and sporting a jaunty Robin Hood-style hat. A pity they hadn't brought William with them, some people remarked in the course of their walkabout. 'We'll bring him next time,' Diana promised them.

The kissing continued. A small boy took momentary advantage of the Princess' preoccupation with the flowers and birthday cards for William which were being pressed upon her to seize her hand and kiss it. In Charlottetown, on Prince Edward Island, a man in the crowd did the same. A young housewife asked Charles for a kiss and got it, even if it was only a token brushing of the cheek by the princely lips. Elsewhere, it was Charles who turned an obliging cheek when a girl asked if she could kiss him. 'It won't do you any good,' he joked.

In some respects perhaps, the tour did not get off to an ideal start. The sunshine of their first day was to be followed by fog and rain—so much rain on one occasion that, for their walkabout, tons of gravel had to be transported and spread to soak up the mud in a local park. That walkabout took place in heavy drizzle. Even so, the Princess insisted on carrying on without either a raincoat or an umbrella for as long as possible and was well soaked by the time she resorted to both. Mist and low cloud caused the cancellation of some engagements necessitating air travel, including one to the small township of Annapolis Royal. 'The Prince won't let us down,' the townsfolk insisted as they turned out to await the anticipated royal arrival. Unfortunately, though it was fine enough in Annapolis Royal, the weather in Halifax was too bad for take-off, and the Prince did.

There were a couple of occasions when, as at his own wedding, Prince Charles rather fluffed his lines. One was at Shelburne, where the royal visit also marked the 200th anniversary of the arrival there of British loyalists forced to flee the United States. The local population turned out to welcome the royal visitors dressed to a man, woman and child in the style of George III. Charles' speech was impromptu and unprepared, so a small slip was perhaps both understandable and forgivable. He was on safe enough ground in saying that he was the first member of the Royal Family ever to go there, but felt he should say something more. 'I hope we can send our son back to mark your—er—tercentenary.' At that point he broke off, amidst chuckles from his audience, realizing a shade too late that little Prince William would have to be a centenarian if he was to do that. The second occasion was in St John, where he made the mistake of saying how delighted he was to be in St John's (which happens to be some five hundred miles away in Newfoundland). Later, apologizing for confusing the two places, he recalled that his father had coined a word—'dontopedaeology'—to describe such slips of the tongue. It is, according to Philip, 'the art of opening your mouth and putting your foot in it'. 'Clearly it's hereditary,' Charles joked.

If Canadians who heard the Prince on these occasions were more amused than affronted by his 'dontopedaeology', he himself was anything but amused by a report in the Halifax *Daily News* of remarks made by his wife during the course of a reception aboard the royal yacht. He was upset, as Diana was also, not because she had been misquoted but by the fact that she was quoted at all. Journalists invited to the reception, which it was hoped would result in establishing a good relationship with the Press at the very start of the tour, were informed in advance that the whole affair would be 'off the record'—meaning that it was a strictly private occasion, with anything said or done not for public consumption. Despite this, the *Daily News*, jointly owned by a British couple, David and Diana Bentley, published a verbatim account of remarks which one Diana made—or was said to have made—to the other during the course of the reception.

Under the somewhat sensational headline 'AGONIES OF A PRINCESS', Diana the princess was quoted as lamenting to Diana the journalist about the way she was treated by some of the tabloid newspapers back home in Britain. 'When they write something horrible, I get a horrible feeling right here,' she was reported as saying, hand touching the region of her heart, 'and I don't want to go outside.' It would probably take her five or ten

years to become accustomed to meeting 'media types', according
to another quote.

Victor Chapman, the royal couple's press officer, lambasted
the report as 'a despicable action' which jeopardized the whole
idea of informal meetings between journalists and members of
the Royal Family. The *Daily News*, he announced, would be
banned from future Press receptions. Diana Bentley thought his
attitude 'a massive over-reaction' while also offering to apologize
if the Princess thought she had been unfair.

Despite such hitches and fluffs early on, the tour, overall, was
to prove every bit as successful as the royal couple's earlier visits
to Australia and New Zealand. The royal yacht *Britannia*,
aboard which they had spent their honeymoon, again did duty
as a floating hotel for their visits to various points along
Canada's eastern seaboard. One of the Prince's first tasks, once
they were settled into their quarters, was to present campaign
medals to twelve members of the crew who had seen service with
the British task force in the South Atlantic. He and the Princess
also posed for a photograph with the gallant dozen.

To the average down-to-earth Canadian, the royal couple
were 'Chuck and Di' rather than Prince and Princess of Wales.
Even Buckingham Palace, with its sometimes rather fussy
attitude to royal names and titles, could hardly disapprove of
home-made placards displaying such heart-warming sentiments
as 'WE LOVE YOU CHUCK AND DI'. So emotional did
things become in St John, where more than fifty thousand
people turned out to greet the couple, that teenage girls and old
ladies alike wept openly and unashamedly in the streets. As in
Australia and New Zealand, it was Diana whom people most
wanted to see. If not all her outfits were brand-new—some had
been worn before in Australia and New Zealand—they were,
whatever some critics might say, as fetching as practicality
permitted. Her hats, for the most part, were stunning. She
declined the offer of a bib to safeguard her dress at one lobster
feast they attended on the grounds that wriggling it over her
head might dislodge her hat. Charles, however, with no hat to
worry about, donned a bib. Both maintained their reputation
for witty banter. 'It's as old as my husband,' said Diana,
displaying mock horror, when one old lady told her that the flag
she was waving dated from Queen Victoria's day. Others were
quick to latch on to this mood of royal humour. Pierre Trudeau,

the Canadian Prime Minister, quipped at a banquet in Halifax that perhaps they should hire the Prince as an official guide for the Princess on this, her first visit to Canada. 'The pay will not be very good,' he said, 'but the company will be very pleasant.'

Trudeau, initially, had not perhaps been too enthusiastic at the prospect of having to cope with yet another royal visit. Understandably. Having to play host to the Prince and Princess meant time spent away from what he may well have regarded as more important matters of government. However, his first meeting with the Princess brought a change of heart. Thereafter he was quick to invite himself to almost every function the couple were due to attend. 'Ask me about her beautiful blue eyes,' he cooed to one seeker after information. Nor was he the only one on whom the Princess seemed to have this sort of effect. 'I guess I'm just falling in love,' sighed Brian Peckford, the Newfoundland Premier, after meeting her. And Richard Hatfield, Premier of New Brunswick, waxed positively lyrical when he found himself proposed a toast to the royal visitors. 'Let the flame burn,' he eulogized, 'to warm hope, to cancel cynicism and despair, to heat the soul that remains and remembers. Yes, let the flame burn. For the flame is love.'

Even Prince Charles, no mean speech-maker himself, seemed rather taken aback by the lyricism and brevity of the toast. 'You have left me almost speechless,' he said in reply. 'I had no idea you were such a poet. Not only that; I thought you were going to speak for much longer. You have done the dirty on me.'

Canadians of less elevated status, women as well as men, teenagers as well as adults, were no less infatuated with the Princess. 'Which side will Diana be on?' was the most important question of the day at each fresh walkabout. Everywhere the couple went, they found themselves showered with birthday gifts for their small son, among them a miniature Indian outfit such as the Queen and Prince Philip were similarly given in Canada for Charles when he was a small boy. In St John alone there were so many flowers and gifts that the half-dozen army women accompanying the couple found their arms full, and reinforcements had to be hastily summoned. In Edmonton so many flowers were given to, thrust at, even thrown to Diana that a whole team of girls was required to collect and carry them. As always, most of them went later to local hospitals, while aboard

Britannia three secretaries worked overtime writing thank-you notes.

As always, of course, security was tight wherever they went. A man in charge of a small group of children waiting to see the royal couple made the mistake of standing with his hands behind his back. He was promptly pounced on by a security man. 'Let's see your hands.' Astonished, he showed them. They were quite empty. Perhaps wisely, the tour itinerary steered clear of Quebec, heartland of French-speaking Canada, where would-be separatists rioted in the streets when the Queen went there in the 1960s. However, by way of a test as to what might be expected if Quebec was included in a later tour of Canada, visits had been arranged to two towns in New Brunswick with large French-speaking populations. The result of these visits, during which the Prince displayed his own ability to speak French, was thought to be 'encouraging'. Encouraging also was the fact that various French-language newspapers gave the royal visit considerable coverage. Commented Claude St Laurent, deputy editor of the main evening news on the French television network: 'I think people are happy with this young couple. Princess Diana has been written about all over the world and it's like having a great celebrity in town. I think she's making quite a hit.'

The period of the tour meant not only that the royal parents were not with their baby son on his first birthday but also that part at least of Diana's birthday would be spent airborne on their way back to Britain. Father's Day also popped up while they were in Canada. Charles sat down to breakfast that morning to find two cards awaiting his attention. One was from his wife and the other supposedly from his small son, who, if he could already say 'Dada' or 'Papa', certainly could not yet write. 'It makes me feel so old,' groaned Father.

While his parents were in Canada, William, back home in Britain, migrated back and forth between his parents' apartment at Kensington Palace and his grandparents' weekend home at Windsor Castle. It was early afternoon at Kensington Palace on 21 June, and a small lunchtime birthday party was in progress, when his parents telephoned from the royal yacht, aboard which it was still eight o'clock in the morning, to wish him a happy birthday. There were two birthday cakes on the table. One had been ordered by Charles from Robert and Paul

Davidson, two Manchester brothers who had been helped to set
up in business by the fund the Prince sponsors to aid enterprising
young people. The other, decorated with nursery-rhyme
characters, had been made by two cooks at the Navy's cookery
school at Chatham, Chief Petty Officers David Avery and
David Scott. 'Make it a sponge cake,' Charles had said when
they offered to make a birthday cake for his son. 'He will find it
easier to eat.'

William received more than a thousand cards on his first
birthday. There were also scores of gifts from members of the
public as well as those from his grandparents, uncles, aunts and
cousins. His parents too had left small gifts to be opened in their
absence, though their main gift would await their return to
Britain so that they could have the pleasure of giving it to him
themselves.

When the telephone rang, Nanny Barnes held it to William's
ear so that he could hear his parents' voices. He responded to
their birthday greetings with what his father described as 'a few
little squeaks'. However, those few little squeaks were sufficient
for his mother, on the other side of the Atlantic, to become
slightly emotional. 'I really am missing him,' she confessed
during the course of a subsequent walkabout in Ottawa amidst
banners saying 'HAPPY BIRTHDAY PRINCE WILLIAM'.
'He is a beautiful little boy and we are both extremely proud of
him.'

Among the places the couple visited during their stay in
Ottawa was the Terry Fox Canadian Youth Centre. Not to be
confused with the sort of youth club to be found back home in
Britain, the Terry Fox Centre is dedicated to teaching young
Canadians more about their national heritage and training
them in the skills of government. Its existence commemorates
the extraordinary exploit of a remarkable young Canadian.
Terrance Stanley Fox was twenty-two when he set out to raise
money for cancer research by running right across Canada, a
daunting marathon even for someone sound in wind and limb.
And Terry Fox was hardly that, a cancer victim himself with an
artificial leg. Sadly, he did not live to complete his self-imposed
marathon, but averaging eighteen miles a day, forced to hop
twice for every step he took with his one good leg, he had covered
an amazing 3,339 miles before he was forced to give up and
return home by ambulance to die. By then he was a national

hero whose exploits brought a staggering $30 million flooding in for cancer research. When Prince Charles, shortly before he married Diana, heard that the Royal Canadian Legion was raising money for a wedding gift, he asked them not to buy anything but to put the money to 'good use'. The result was a cheque for $227,000 which was handed over on behalf of Charles and Diana to buy furniture and equipment for the Centre which remembers Terry Fox and his courageous exploit. 'Such extraordinary courage and determination are a great example to us all,' Prince Charles said as he and the Princess planted a commemorative tree in the grounds of the Centre.

With the royal yacht anchored in Conception Bay (which doubtless afforded Charles a further opportunity to tease his wife on the subject of more children), the couple went ashore in Newfoundland to join in the celebrations marking the 400th anniversary of the claiming of the island in the name of the first Elizabeth. As part of the celebrations Charles opened a youth festival and presented new colours to the local regiment. Together, they listened to folk music and, with the help of song sheets, joined enthusiastically in the singing of some rollicking sea-shanties. They climbed Cape Spear, Canada's most easterly point, and were amused, just short of the summit, to find themselves confronted by a signpost pointing to: Buckingham Palace, 4,750 kilometres. During their walk on the headland, in an attempt to eavesdrop on Diana's conversation with people in the crowd, a television boom microphone was infiltrated in the vicinity of her legs. 'Do that again and I'll kick it,' she threatened. The incident did nothing to mar the new-found love affair between the Princess and the Canadian people. 'They are both fantastic, super people,' said the Newfoundland Premier. 'I didn't realize they would be so down to earth and so easy to get to know. The Princess is very witty too.'

Wittiness was evident when the Premier told Diana that he and his wife had two daughters and were now hoping to have a son. 'That's your problem, not mine,' she rejoined, laughing. More seriously, she confided that initially she had found it difficult to cope with the pressures of royal life. 'But I have learned a lot in the past three or four months,' she added, 'and feel that I am doing my job better now than I was before.'

Most Canadians she met would have said that she was under-estimating herself. They thought she did her job superbly, with cheerfulness, compassion and sensitivity. Visiting a local hospital, she took the time to sit on every single bed and chat with its occupant. 'I was struck by her really soft spot for people who are sick or disabled,' said the Newfoundland Premier. This 'soft spot' was particularly evident during a visit to Harbour Grace. A small boy presented her with a bouquet. She accepted it, bent to thank him and moved on. It was only later that she learned from the Premier, Brian Peckford, that the boy was blind. 'She almost cried when I told her,' he recalls. Later, at a civic luncheon, the Princess spotted the boy again and made an immediate beeline for him. Let the boy himself, Edward Barnes, tell the rest of the story.

'She told me she was wearing a thick blue coat. She took my hand and put the material in it so that I could feel it. She guided my hand to the big buttons on it. She let me touch her shoes and leg. She took both of my hands in hers and came so close I could have touched her face, but I was too nervous. She told me I had done a good job with the flowers and then she talked to my Mom and Dad.' She also asked Edward if he would like a kiss. But he was too nervous of that. 'No,' he said. Diana laughed. 'Perhaps he's a bit young to be kissing girls,' she joked with his parents.

On Prince Edward Island, Canada's smallest province, they were fed with lobster and serenaded with fiddles and ukuleles. A trotting race staged in their honour attracted entries from all parts of Canada, with Charles presenting a prize blanket to the winning horse. Leaving *Britannia* behind, they journeyed across Canada to Alberta, where an hotel suite in Edmonton had been refurbished for them at a cost of $30,000. As if that was still not sufficient, art work estimated to be worth $1 million was brought in to adorn the walls. Highlight of their stay in Alberta was a barbecue at Fort Edmonton, a reconstruction of the original nineteenth-century settlement. 'Dress semi-formal, Klondike era,' read the invitations. Forewarned is forearmed, and the royal couple entered wholeheartedly into the spirit of the occasion with outfits they had had made in London and taken to Canada with them. Diana wore a bustle dress of pink silk and cream lace with matching hat and high lace-up boots while Charles copied the outfit his great-great-grandfather had worn when he visited Canada in 1860, frock coat and striped trousers, winged collar, silk cravat and spats, with a silver-topped cane to add an extra touch of elegance. On their insistence, their entourage of private secretary, Press secretary and two detectives also dressed in vintage outfits which would blend with the hired crinolines and fancy waistcoats of the local 'Klondikers'.

With Press and television cameras banned from the raunchy cabaret staged for their entertainment in a marquee which carried the legend 'Kelly's Saloon', Prince and Princess for once could afford to let their hair down somewhat. 'Oh, no,' Diana called out, glancing sideways at her husband and shaking her head in vigorous disagreement, when Klondike Kate (who is Gillian Campbell in real life) demanded to know from the stage, 'Isn't it true, gels, that a good man is hard to find?' Alderman Ronald Hayter, who was sitting at the Prince's table, found himself enticed onto the stage and induced to waggle his rear end in time to Kate's raucous singing. 'I'm glad it was you and not me,' Charles joked as the worthy alderman returned to his seat. Though he did not know it, the Prince had had a narrow escape. The original idea had been to lure him on stage to join 'Kate' in a routine which would have ended with him being given one of her garters. However, some thought this might be taking things a little too far, and so Charles was let off. As it was, he and Diana thoroughly enjoyed the whole show, which included a can-can routine by four blondes in scarlet leotards and fishnet tights, though Charles seemed nervous when it came to standing up, linking hands and joining in a robust chorus of 'Daisy, Daisy'. Diana, already on her feet and singing enthusiastically, flashed him an encouraging smile and he joined in too.

That particular royal shindig was held the evening before Diana's twenty-second birthday. Alberta time being several hours behind Greenwich, some people calculated that it was already her birthday in London, if not in Edmonton, and her first birthday gift was handed to her on her way to the barbecue. Her birthday proper brought a shower of further gifts, including jewellery from Charles, lots of flowers, loads of cards and birthday greetings from her royal in-laws, the Queen in London, England, and Prince Philip, at that time in London, Ontario. And even the Queen Mother has never had 'Happy Birthday' sung to her by such a vast crowd. Some 62,000 young athletes from ninety-five countries joined in the vocal tribute to her when, with her husband, she attended the opening ceremony of the World University Games.

It made a fitting and exciting conclusion to a tour which, despite a few upsets at the outset, both Prince and Princess had thoroughly enjoyed. Said Charles, before they flew back to Britain, 'We have both been overwhelmed by the kindness we have come across during our visit. "Overwhelmed" is almost an understatement. We have been spoilt thoroughly by the enthusiasm of people's quite extraordinary warmth. We have both been greatly touched, and I know my wife has been enormously moved by the wealth of love and affection which has surrounded her.'

What little was left of the Princess' twenty-second birthday was spent aboard a Canadian Air Force jet winging the couple back to Britain. Naturally, there had to be a birthday party. It was held thirty thousand feet up. There was champagne to drink and, like her small son, Diana had the choice of two birthday cakes. One, from the crew of the aircraft, was inscribed 'Love From Canada'. But it was the other which surely came closest to her heart. Made to the order of her husband while they were in Edmonton, its sugar-iced legend consisted of four words: 'I Love You, Darling.'

13 A Personal Question

Much as they had enjoyed the greater part of their Canadian tour, the royal parents were naturally delighted to be home again and reunited with their baby son. There was the fun of helping him to celebrate his first birthday all over again and witnessing his delight at the gift they had not been around to give him on his birthday proper. It was just as well perhaps that it was 'something he can't break', for William was fast turning from a baby into a small boy, or at least a toddler, and a lively and energetic one at that. He was getting to be 'quite a handful', Diana confided.

Small children, once they can get around under their own steam, are inclined to be inquisitive, and so it was with William. Intrigued by a small coloured button fixed to the nursery wall at Balmoral, when they went there on holiday a few weeks later, he prodded it with an inquiring finger. The result was to trigger off the castle security system, with armed detectives, police dogs and patrol cars alerted and springing briefly into action. William's nanny revealed what had happened, and the alert was called off.

Diana, in particular, was determined to enjoy what yet remained of William's babyhood to the full, though her ever-expanding role as Princess of Wales more and more interfered with the joys of motherhood. Only when parents and baby escaped to Highgrove or when they were on holiday at Balmoral could she be a fulltime mother, taking William for outings in the grounds, teaching him to feed himself at mealtimes and tucking him up at night. Charles too enjoyed spending time with his small son, particularly the splashing fun of baby's bath-time. 'He is a doting daddy and does everything perfectly,' Diana confided, though Charles himself sometimes found fatherhood rather different from what he had imagined. In his bachelor days he was sometimes known to pontificate on how children should be brought up. Now that he had a child of his own, he discovered more and more that theory does not always work in practice; that small children have wills of their own. 'Suddenly you find that your child is not a malleable object or an offprint of yourself, but the culmination of goodness knows how many thousands of years and genetic make-up in your ancestors,' he was obliged to concede.

Charles himself was brought up to the axiom that politeness is the essence of princedom. From an early age he was taught to say 'Please' and 'Thank you', to ask if he wanted something and not simply help himself, to treat everyone, including servants, with consideration and respect. So there was an echo of his own upbringing in his views on how William, and any brothers or sisters William might yet have, should be brought up. 'I would like to bring up our children to be well-mannered,' he said, 'to think of other people, to put themselves into other people's positions, to do unto others as they would have done unto them. At the end of it, even if they are not very bright or very qualified, at least if they have reasonable manners they will get much further in life than by not having them.'

Significantly, in interviews, speeches, conversation, he continued constantly to refer to 'our children' rather than 'our child' or 'our son'. A psychologist might have deduced that, with his thirty-fifth birthday now visible on the horizon of time, Charles was anxious to have more children while he was still of an age fully to enjoy being a father to them. His wife was perhaps a shade less eager to continue with what Charles calls 'the breeding programme'. Thrilled as she was with William, much as she doted on him, she had not exactly enjoyed her months of pregnancy. Nor, perhaps, was she desirous of sacrificing her figure again quite so soon and again going through the struggle of getting it back. While Charles may have been of the opinion that 12-15 months was the ideal age-gap between first and second children—there are in fact twenty-one months between himself and Princess Anne—Diana was perhaps more inclined to share the views of the royal gynaecologist that 12-18 months after the birth of a first baby is time enough for a young mother to become pregnant again. And as subsequent events have shown, even that spacing was to be exceeded by several months.

Diana's figure at this time, with William just turned a year old, was of model-girl proportions. Almost as though the rigours of yet another royal tour had brought out the best in her, she returned to Britain from Canada looking 'young, charming and beautiful'. The words are those of the American designer Richard Blackwell, high praise indeed from a self-appointed arbiter of feminine beauty who a year before had taken it upon himself to criticize the Princess for looking like 'a bathing beauty out of a 1910 silent movie' and putting her top of his list of 'the World's Worst Dressed Women'. Now, seeing her again shortly after the couple's return from Canada, he said of her, 'She has gone through the whole metamorphosis and dresses now as an independent young woman.'

Still wary of the Press (and the betrayal of her confidence by the Halifax *Daily News* had hardly helped in this respect), Diana, though she never stopped talking about William in private, declined to be interviewed on the subject of his upbringing—or, indeed, on any other topic, preferring to leave that sort of thing to her more experienced husband. But an offguard remark during a visit to Elmhurst Ballet School provided a revealing insight into her own childhood. As a girl, she had once dreamed of becoming a ballet dancer, she said. But, sadly, she grew too tall.

The ballet school visit was only one in a busy round of public engagements awaiting the couple's return from Canada, their public paths diverging more and more as the Princess steadily developed a public life of her own. There was, for instance, a solo visit to open an extension to a toy factory in Peterlee from which she returned with a portable toy-box for William to take with him on any future royal tours he might undertake with mum and dad. While in Peterlee she was also given a large box of fruit by a shopkeeper fan. 'It's heavy,' the shopkeeper cautioned her. 'Don't worry,' she replied. 'I'm a strong girl.'

While the Princess was in Peterlee, Charles was in North Wales. The day before he had been in East Anglia and, forgoing the fun of William's bath-time, had stayed on to attend a dinner given by the Cambridge Commonwealth Trust in the familiar surroundings of Trinity College where he had once been a student. A day or so later, with Charles again away, this time visiting some of his Duchy of Cornwall holdings as well as attending the first meeting of the Duchy's Advisory Group on Archaeology, a subject in which he is keenly interested, the Princess travelled to Northampton to open a new psychiatric unit at St Andrew's Hospital. Northampton being so close to Althorp, her family's seat, it was an affectionate gesture on her part to invite her father to be with her at the opening ceremony.

Prince Charles, in an interview published around this time, had something to say on his attitude to his role as Prince of Wales. 'I can only go muddling along,' he said, 'pursuing the sort of things I think are right and true, and hope there's a result. I'm not somebody overburdened with a sense of self-confidence about such things. I always feel that I should be some-what reticent, otherwise you end up thinking you are more important than you are. I just go on trying to encourage, trying to help.'

However, there are some subjects on which he is less reticent than others. Alternative medicine is one. Like his mother and grandmother, the Queen and the Queen Mother, he believes that modern drugs and surgery are not the be-all and end-all of medical practice. 'Think positively,' he advised Michael Bentine's younger daughter in a letter when she was ill with cancer. So it was perhaps not surprising, shortly after he and the Princess returned from Canada, to find him opening the new premises of the Cancer Help Centre in Bristol. His invitation to open the centre followed upon an address he had given at the 150th anniversary dinner of the British Medical Association. The views he aired on that occasion were also contained in a written message delivered to the Association's annual meeting while he was away in Canada.

'Sophistication is only skin deep,' the Prince wrote in his message, 'and when it comes to healing people it seems to me that account has to be taken of those sometimes long-neglected complementary methods of medicine which, in the right hands, can bring considerable relief, if not hope, to an increasing number of people. I hope that, while maintaining and improving the standards with which the Association is so rightly concerned, the medical profession will at the same time keep a corner of its mind open enough to admit those shafts of light which can preserve that sense of paradox so vital to our sense of unity with nature.'

However, his decision to open the Cancer Self Help Centre, with its controversial programme of physical, emotional and spiritual therapy, was not without critics. 'I do feel strongly about the Prince of Wales making a royal tour of something so full of bogus notions,' said one medical critic, while the Cancer Aftercare and Rehabilitation Society was later to write to the Prince insisting that the Centre's methods were 'speculative and unproven'.

Charles, in his opening speech, set out to counter such criticisms. 'The great value, it seems to me, of the type of treatment provided here,' he said, 'is not that extravagant claims are made on its part, but that it does no positive harm to the patient. Far from it. For so much depends on marshalling the psychological and spiritual forces of the patient to tackle the appalling afflictions that have arisen. . . . Such an approach might be given a number of descriptions such as psychotherapy or religion or the power of prayer. But it represents that invisible aspect of this universe which, although unproved in terms of orthodox science as man has devised it, nevertheless cries out for us to keep our minds as open as possible and not to dismiss it as mere hocus-pocus.' He felt, he said, that it was only right that 'a patient should be free to try a different form of treatment if he or she feels that little progress is being made in, for instance, what could be referred to as drug-based healing.'

During his tour of the Centre, the Prince talked with patients, watched meditation classes in progress, sat in on counselling and therapy sessions, inspected the kitchens where the raw vegetable diets which form part of the treatment are prepared, and submitted himself to the scrutiny of a bio-feedback machine. The results of the test showed him to be 'very calm and relaxed', though his detective bodyguard, Inspector Colin Trimming, who also took the test, was found to be 'in a state of stress'.

If Charles is perhaps more like his mother than his father in personality, there seemed to be an ever-louder echo of Prince Philip developing in his speech-making. The Queen, because she is Queen, is limited mainly to mouthing platitudes which, if they do not excite or enthuse, do not arouse controversy either. Prince Philip can afford to be more outspoken. He is a man who believes in speaking out, whether or not it arouses controversy or attracts criticism. More and more it seems that his eldest son is taking after him in this connection, even to the point of sailing fairly close to the political wind from which members of the Royal Family are traditionally supposed to steer clear in their speech-making. Another speech around this time, delivered to an audience of chief constables, found the Prince exhorting

Britain's politicians to consider new ways of treating the increasing number of young offenders.

'The experience I have had over the past ten years,' he told his Police Foundation audience, 'is that if the young are placed in a disciplined environment—perhaps the first time they have ever known what it is like—presented with challenging circumstances and pushed beyond themselves, the results can be quite extraordinary. Suddenly they find hidden corners in their characters which they never knew existed. They develop talents and gifts which would otherwise never have materialized. They develop a self-confidence and a self-reliance that above all is the essential quality necessary to escape from a cycle of deprivation or alienation within an urban and artificial environment.'

In fact, the Prince's experience of discipline and challenge go back rather more than merely ten years. It started at the tender age of nine when, on his father's insistence, he was uprooted from the cottonwool confines of the royal schoolroom and bundled off to boarding school. Gordonstoun, in particular, presented him with a whole series of challenges which began the process of changing him from the shy, self-conscious child he was to the confident, outspoken man he has become. A spell of schooling in Australia, where he was labelled 'a pommie bastard', posed yet more challenges. So did his time at Cambridge University and five years in the Royal Navy. And perhaps the biggest challenge of all has been the need to live up to what others expect of him.

He mentioned none of this in his speech. What he did mention instead was a series of courses for some two thousand youngsters organized by the armed forces at Fort George, near Inverness. He had visited Fort George to see something of the scheme for himself, he said, and thought the youngsters taking part had benefited 'immeasurably'.

'Although none of them were offenders,' he went on, 'I believe that a similar approach with offenders, perhaps coupled with an initial detention sentence, could replace an element of that lost humanity which is so vital to our self-esteem and without which we have little compassion or feeling for anyone else around us. But it needs to be brought out, in most cases, through being made to do things they may not want to do by people who know the art of leading, motivating and pushing.'

Predictably perhaps, it was a speech which, like many made

by his father, attracted not a little criticism from left-wingers. Typical was a comment made by Frank Allaun, a member of the Labour Party's National Executive Committee. 'Dangerous nonsense', he labelled the Prince's views. 'Young people want jobs, not military training. Royalty in Britain are expected to keep out of politics. They should do so, as does the Queen.'

If their royal duties often contrive to separate Charles and Diana, they still manage to see more of each other than many another married couple, publicly as well as privately. They were together around this time at a banquet in aid of the Children of Poland Appeal, at a reception they gave at Kensington Palace for people involved in community relations, at a luncheon for members of the Prince's Council, at another luncheon organized by the Variety Club of Great Britain, at a Buckingham Palace garden party which, with Britain sweltering in a heatwave, Diana graced with bare legs, and most lovingly together at Smith's Lawn, Windsor, where she again watched her husband play polo. They were together too at a rock concert in aid of the Prince of Wales Trust. The concert featured Duran Duran, a group whose music both enjoy, though Diana's favourite group is—or was then, according to her answer to a question posed during her visit to Northampton—Supertramp.

Another brief parting saw the couple embark on journeys which, though separate, were calculated to evoke old memories for both. Diana's trip took her back to the district where she spent her early childhood, to King's Lynn where she first went to school. So it was very much a sentimental journey even if she no longer remembers going there as a very small girl—she was barely two at the time—to see her grandmother, Ruth, Lady Fermoy, granted the Freedom of the Borough. Consequently, she was in lighthearted mood. 'Where did you escape from?' she asked a small boy with a skinhead haircut. 'It's very noble of you to stay away from your televisions just to see me,' she joked with others in the crowd. A host of relatives and old friends were there to greet her, among them her Fermoy grandmother and her godmother, Lady Mary Colman, whose husband is Lord Lieutenant of Norfolk. There were brief reunions with her old headmistress, Jean Lowe, and a childhood friend, Henry Bellingham, Member of Parliament for North West Norfolk. The purpose of her visit was to attend the opening concert of the town's annual arts festival, and a relative by marriage, the Duke of Kent, joined her in the audience. The Duchess of Kent, convalescent after her recent operation, was singing in the concert with the Bach Choir. So, to Diana's delight, was Carolyn Pride, now Carolyn Bartholomew, one of her former flatmates.

Charles, meantime, was in Aberystwyth, presiding over a meeting of the governors of the University College of Wales (where he himself was briefly a student in the run-up to his investiture as Prince of Wales). In the fourteen years since, things had not changed all that much, it seemed. As in 1969, his arrival was greeted by jeering from a handful of students professing to see him as a symbol of English imperialism.

The couple's second wedding anniversary, 29 July, was kept carefully free from official engagements. However, the fact did not prevent them from appearing together in public. Looking every inch a married couple still head over heels in love with each other, they journeyed together to Cowdray Park, where Charles played polo while Diana watched. To make up for his 'day off', Charles was back on royal duty the following day, a Saturday, travelling to South Wales in his capacity as Colonel of the Welsh Guards to receive the freedom of Merthyr Tydfil on behalf of the regiment which had suffered the worst casualties of any during the brief but bloody campaign to regain the Falkland Islands.

Another visit around this time was to Stoke Mandeville. It had been arranged originally that Charles would go there alone to open a new spinal injuries centre. To the surprise and delight of everyone associated with the project, Diana arrived with him, sitting on beds to chat with disabled patients and even calling her husband back when she realized that he had failed to notice Sergeant-Major Kenneth Yeomans, a member of the Red Devils parachute team, in hospital with a broken back which he had sustained in helping another member of the team whose parachute failed to open.

There were various explanations to account for Diana's unexpected appearance. It was 'a complicated way of getting a record played on Radio One', joked television star Jimmy Savile, who had masterminded the raising of the £10 million required to build the new centre. Charles himself said, 'I was telling her about this marvellous place and she insisted on seeing it for herself.' And perhaps there was also another, more personal reason, a desire on Diana's part to stay close to her husband in the light of recent events. Only twenty-four hours before, police in nearby Aylesbury had arrested a man who was later charged with threatening to kill the Prince.

Their royal duty done in so many different directions, in Australia, New Zealand and Canada as well as Britain, it was time for the couple to enjoy another well-deserved rest. Taking William with them, and with Charles himself at the controls of their aircraft, they flew north to join the rest of the Royal Family on holiday at Balmoral. But even at Balmoral it was not to be all play and no work. Mindful of previous criticism that she had been seen little in Scotland, the Princess interrupted her holiday from time to time to carry out public engagements in Dundee, Coatbridge and elsewhere.

Leaving her husband behind, she also paid a flying visit to London, curiously reminiscent of those flying excursions between Balmoral and London two years earlier. Those trips had been followed by the announcement of her pregnancy. Coincidentally or otherwise, this latest visit to London also came on the day that George Pinker, the royal gynaecologist, was due back from holiday. Speculation was inevitable. The trip to London was 'purely a private matter', Buckingham Palace insisted. So is pregnancy, of course, and the palace Press office found itself bombarded with newspaper inquiries. Was the Princess expecting another baby? In May? In April? 'If and when the Princess was pregnant, she would make her own announcement,' said the palace, stoically.

Some people were not prepared to wait for that. When Diana went to Dundee a few days later, a girl working in a marmalade and confectionery factory she visited posed the pointblank question: 'Is it true that you are expecting another baby?'

'That is a very personal question,' the Princess replied, blushing.

Another girl, one of a crowd outside the factory gates, tried a slightly more oblique approach. 'If you are pregnant, would you prefer a boy or a girl?' she asked. However, that did not work either. 'That is a very personal question,' the Princess said again, smiling with embarrassment.

More and more she was mastering the subtlety required of royalty in this era of open communication. If, by turning defence into attack, she contrived to be a girl who didn't say Yes and didn't say No in Dundee, she also managed to avoid a somewhat less obvious pitfall in Coatbridge where she visited a training workshop. To the intense disappointment of several hopeful photographers, she neatly sidestepped that area of the workshop where babies' cradles were being made. And all her new-found expertise was called into play the day she flew south from Balmoral to visit a school for mentally handicapped children in Bedfordshire. She was talking to the school's principal when a small girl stretched out a hand to touch her in the region of her tummy. Diana looked down and could scarcely believe her ears when the child asked her, 'How's your baby then?' For a moment the Princess looked taken aback. Then she laughed. 'Did I hear right?' she asked, turning embarrassment into a joke. The question came up yet again when she and Charles visited a hospital for disabled servicemen in Strathclyde. It was an ex-sailor there who posed the question: 'Is there another on the way?' Again the Princess laughed it off, so infectiously that everyone else in the ward joined in the laughter, and laughter avoided the necessity for a straight answer.

If his parents were obliged to interrupt their Balmoral holiday from time to time to fulfil public engagements, William was not. Nevertheless, at sixteen months, he was already sufficiently versed in the ways of royalty to smile and wave at the photographers waiting at Aberdeen Airport to picture the family's departure when they flew south again for the winter. That there was to be no baby brother or sister for William as early as the spring of 1984 became increasingly clear as his mother embarked upon a fresh spate of public engagements, now sufficiently numerous to necessitate her having her own equerry in the person of Lieutenant-Commander Peter Eberle. 'She's never pregnant; she's thin as a rake,' said female wiseacres who glimpsed her at the various functions she attended following the couple's return from Balmoral. With Charles, she went to a Barry Manilow concert at London's Festival Hall, a charity performance of *Hay Fever* at the Queen's Theatre and another concert by the Spanish singer Placido Domingo. On her own, she opened a new block at the London Chest Hospital and the West Indian Family Centre in Brixton where a small West Indian girl briefly stole the show with her delightful hip-wriggling, hand-clapping accompaniment to a Caribbean calypso.

In fulfilment of a promise made to her former Colherne Court flatmates, the Princess was among the wedding guests when another of them married that October. This time the bride was Anne Bolton, the girl with whom Diana had been briefly united during her Australian tour earlier in the year. Indeed, it was during that 'Down Under' trip that Anne met and fell in love with Noel Hill, the Australian she married. Also among the wedding guests were the former Carolyn Pride, now Mrs William Bartholomew, whose wedding the Princess had also attended, and Virginia Pitman, the only one of the 'Famous Four' still unwed.

Charles equally had his own busy round of engagements, meetings, luncheons, dinners, plus a brief visit to the Scilly Isles which form part of the Duchy of Cornwall. Along with his wife and brothers, he was present to see his mother unveil a statue of his 'honorary grandfather', the murdered Mountbatten of Burma. He and Diana were also together at a memorial service to the men of the Welsh Guards who had been killed in the Falklands and at the annual British Legion Festival of Remembrance. Remembrance Day again saw the Princess watching from a balcony in Whitehall while the Prince, deputizing for the Queen, who was away in Kenya, laid a wreath at the Cenotaph. But she did not go with him that afternoon to the Remembrance Day service in the Guards Chapel.

The following day, 14 November, was Charles' thirty-fifth birthday. Rumour had it that he would mark the day by announcing that he and Diana were expecting another child, but again rumour turned out to be no more than wishful thinking. The fact that she would not be going with Charles to Brunei in February did not imply that she might be expecting a second child, Buckingham Palace said (though by then, she was).

It addition to public engagements, as November ran its course, Diana also embarked on a number of private shopping expeditions. 'I always like to do my Christmas shopping before the rush starts,' she said. By Christmas William would be a toddler of eighteen months and the toys she bought for him could now be more suited to a small boy than a mere baby. How he was coming along was revealed midway through December when, doubtfully at first but more cheekily later, he joined his parents in the walled garden of their London home at Kensington Palace for another photo-call. Initially he had to be headed off by his father and brought back as he tried to stage a getaway through the garden gate, but later he toddled up and down the line of clicking cameramen like a prince reviewing his troops, smiled to display his eleven teeth and, as a finale, again performed his Maori tongue-poking act. His height was given as 2 feet 10 inches which one baby expert calculated would see him as the tallest of the Royal Family when he grew to manhood. 'He's getting to be quite a handful,' his mother confided in the course of one of her royal walkabouts. He certainly proved to be 'a handful' the day, toddling about the garden with no photographers present, he toddled right through an infra-red beam and again activated the royal security system.

William's photo-call appearance saw a lot of mothers dashing out in an attempt to outfit their own offspring in similar navy-blue snowsuits with embroidered ABC motifs. The majority were disappointed, however. Only a few dozen of the suits had been imported from France and most were already sold by the time pictures of William appeared in print. However, copy-cat manufacturers were quick to take advantage of the situation, craftily stitching similar ABC motifs on their own children's snowsuits in the hope of benefiting from the sudden demand. William, as he goes through the various stages of childhood, is clearly going to be of the same advantage to the manufacturers of children's clothing as his mother is to the more adult fashion trade. An earlier picture of him in an embroidered romper suit had resulted in such a demand for similar outfits that a Derbyshire factory not only re-opened after being forced to close by the recession, but looked optimistically forward to doubling its original work-force.

The weekend before Christmas found the family back at Highgrove. To get the 1983 festive season off to a good start, Charles and Diana invited friends and neighbours to the house to join them in a carol service led by the choir from Westonbirt Girls' School. Sadly, that same day was also the day when five people were killed (with another dying later) and over ninety injured when the IRA planted a car bomb in Hans Crescent at the rear of Harrods. Charles and Diana promptly returned to London to visit the injured in hospital. 'How's William?' one of the injured, Police Sergeant Christopher Stanger, asked Diana. 'He's huge,' she told him. 'He has a healthy appetite—just like his father.'

'What do you feed him on?' asked Stanger's wife, who was there at the time. 'He looks like the Michelin man.'

The royal visits to the two hospitals involved, St Thomas's and the Westminster, were specially arranged to coincide with visiting hours so that the couple could also meet relatives of the injured. 'I understand your suffering,' Charles told one of them and recalled how his great-uncle, Earl Mountbatten of Burma, had also been murdered by the IRA. To the American parents of Mark McDonald, who had flown the Atlantic to be at the bedside of their injured son, the Prince said, 'I apologize on behalf of London.'

Shirking nothing, the Prince and Princess visited even those who were so terribly injured that they were in the intensive care unit. Charles, in particular, was looking pale and distraught when their visit was finally over. 'I think it is extraordinary,' he said, 'that people quite cold-bloodedly can plan an operation like that, knowing the sort of effect it is going to have. It is extraordinary that somebody could have the mentality to do such things. It is very sad. I believe that, ultimately, God is their judge.'

Christmas was again spent at Windsor Castle with others of the Royal Family. The Queen likes nothing so much as to have as many of her family as possible—sons, daughter, grandchildren and others—around her at Christmas. The previous year William had been too young to appreciate Christmas. But now, as 1983 neared its end, he was of an age to experience for the first time the magic of Christmas, gazing wide-eyed at the fairy lights on the tall Christmas tree and, with a little help from his parents, enjoying the excitement of opening his many presents, among them a bulging Christmas stocking home-made by his royal grandmother.

As usual, the Queen and Prince Philip journeyed from Windsor to Sandringham for the New Year. But, this time, Charles and Diana did not go with them, though William did. Prince and Princess had other plans in mind, among them another stab at a winter holiday on the ski slopes of Europe. As any granny would, the Queen happily offered to take charge of William while they were away. Naturally, they travelled to Sandringham to say goodbye to him before leaving on holiday, flying on from there to Zurich in an Andover of the Queen's Flight. Charles himself did the piloting.

Some ninety photographers, from France, Germany, Switzerland and elsewhere as well as Britain, were lined up to record their arrival in Zurich. Diana skipped nimbly down the aircraft steps, looking decidedly non-pregnant and sporting an exotic new hair-style, every inch the holiday princess in red boots and snug-fitting grey trousers, a rainbow-striped sweater and a mohair jacket. Charles, more soberly dressed in a lounge suit and formal topcoat, looked more like a business executive arriving for an important conference. A ninety-minute car drive brought them to Liechtenstein, to the castle home of Prince Hans Adam which was again to be their holiday base.

Their earlier attempt at a winter skiing holiday, a year previous, had turned out an unmitigated disaster. Diana had blamed the Press photographers who hounded them so continuously; the photographers—some of them, at least—had blamed her for refusing to co-operate. Charles had been caught in the middle. This time, in an attempt to obtain privacy during the rest of the holiday, the couple made themselves available for a photo session on their first day out on the snow slopes. Charles was his usual easy-going self. 'Do you want us to fall over?' he quipped at the photographers as cameras clicked and whirred. Diana, though she laughed at one point of the proceedings, looked a shade more apprehensive about the whole business, or perhaps resentful. The cameras continued to click as the two of them positioned themselves to be scooped up by the chair-lift and were borne away. 'A very good goodbye,' Charles called back, hopefully.

'The Prince and Princess have agreed to the photo session at the request of the media,' said a prior statement from Buckingham Palace issued on the couple's behalf, 'and will expect the remainder of their holiday to be considered private with no intrusive activity by any member of the media.'

It was perhaps expecting too much. 'European cameramen do not feel they are bound by any agreement reached between Buckingham Palace and the British Press', commented a Swiss photographer and even some London newspapers were not necessarily willing to commit themselves to accepting what they regarded as a rather unilateral royal declaration. A small example of 'intrusive activity' occurred that same afternoon when a German photographer tried to take a picture of Diana as she met momentary disaster and sprawled full-length in the snow. Whether he succeeded or not will never be known. He was intercepted by police and his film was either confiscated or voluntarily handed over, according to viewpoint.

Diana, as she skied—and sometimes tumbled—on Europe's snow slopes at the beginning of 1984, was again pregnant, even if it was to be another two or three weeks before her own suspicions were fully confirmed. Among the first to know was her brother, Viscount Althorp. She told him when they had lunch together one day shortly before she flew to Oslo to watch a performance of *Carmen* by the London City Ballet of which she is patron. She told her old friend Carolyn Bartholomew (née Pride) when she called at Diana's Kensington Palace apartment and she also telephoned the news to her divorced parents, contriving to catch her mother just as she was about to leave for Australia. In company with Charles, she also told his parents. They couldn't be more delighted, they said.

The trip to Norway was her second solo engagement overseas. The first had been the funeral of Princess Grace in Monaco, a sad occasion. Oslo, by contrast, was fun. If you can't make it as a ballet dancer yourself because you grow too tall, what better than to have your own pet ballet company? Letters from Harold King, the South African-born dancer who founded the company, had earlier lured the Princess along to watch the dancers practise in their rehearsal rooms at Covent Garden; to sit and chat with them over coffee.

'She was terribly interested to know what the work was like, what a ballet dancer's life was like', Harold King recalls. 'And desperately keen to become involved.'

So keen that she became the patron of this small, struggling, talented outfit operating on a commercial shoestring. Just before Christmas she turned up again at the rehearsal rooms to watch a rehearsal of *Carmen*. 'I must see you perform it on stage', she said. Told that all the 1984 performances would be overseas, she arranged to fly to Oslo to see the performance there.

After watching the production, she went backstage to congratulate members of the company before joining some 140 others for supper at the residence of the British ambassador, William Bentley. She stayed overnight with Crown Prince Harald and Princess Sonja, and planted a commemorative tree before flying back to Britain the following morning. A day later, with the official announcement that a small playmate would be joining William in the royal nursery in September, came understanding of why she had seemed somewhat camera-shy during that visit to Oslo and her seeming desire to dodge the photographers on her return to London. It was 14 February— St Valentine's day—when the official announcement appeared in print and doubtless the valentine card Charles gave his wife contained some joking reference to the second baby about which he had teased her so often.

As when she was pregnant with Prince William, Diana planned to continue with public engagements for as long as possible, she said. Two days later, with Charles, she visited the Jaguar car plant in Coventry. Workers there had their own joke prepared, a banner bearing the greeting 'HELLO MOM'. And the ever-joking Charles found himself hoist with his own petard for once. A husband who jokes about 'the breeding programme', as Charles has done in the past, is inviting trouble with a comment to car-workers such as 'Your production here is going very well.'

It was too good an opportunity for shop-floor wit Terry McCauley to miss. 'Your own production line is going well too', he shot back at the Prince.

For once it was Charles who blushed.

14   Crystal Gazing

At some unknown point in time in the years ahead, Prince
Charles will cease to be Prince of Wales and become King
Charles III—unless, of course, he decides to perpetuate the
kingly name borne by his maternal grandfather and great-
grandfather and become King George VII. The choice will be
his. He can cling to his own name, as his mother remained
Elizabeth when she succeeded to the throne, or change to
another, as his grandfather changed from Albert to George
when he became King.

Whatever name he decides to take when the time comes, the
young woman who is now Princess of Wales will then become
Queen Consort. And Prince William will automatically succeed
to his father's title and inheritance as Duke of Cornwall. But he
will not automatically inherit his father's premier title as Prince
of Wales. That title is bestowed, not inherited, and the question
of when it should be bestowed will be a matter for his father.

All this, of course, may be a long way in the future. It could be
another forty years before he became King, Charles himself said
in 1975. Even that, clearly, was no more than a guess, but should
it prove correct, Charles will be a venerable prince in his late
sixties when he finally ascends the throne, which would make
him even older than his great-great-grandfather, King Edward
VII, was when he succeeded the octogenarian Queen Victoria.

The great-great-grandfather who eventually became King
Edward VII passed the long years of waiting as a playboy
prince. Partly this was because it was in his nature to be so and
partly it was because his mother, the autocratic Queen Victoria,
denied him his full and proper place in the royal scheme of
things. The attitude of the present Queen towards her eldest son
is very different from that of her great-great-grandmother
towards hers. Queen Victoria saw the son she called Bertie as
both 'dissolute' and a possible threat to her autocracy. Prince
Charles is certainly not dissolute, and his mother does not see

him as a rival to her sovereignty. On the contrary, ever since he came of age she has trained him along the path of future monarchy, as her own father trained her.

There has been discussion at times as to whether the Queen might one day shorten her son's spell as King-in-waiting by a decision to abdicate, as Queen Juliana of the Netherlands and her mother before her did. But for the Queen to abdicate while her health permits her to continue as sovereign would be to diminish one of the few remaining values of constitutional monarchy. The longer a monarch reigns, the more important she or he becomes to the nation. Governments and prime ministers come and go, ushered in and out by popular vote. The monarch is not dependent upon popular vote but remains to serve as a link between one government and the next, one prime minister and the next, even one generation and the next.

As heir to the throne, Prince Charles' role in the constitutional life of the nation is undefined, and perhaps indefinable. Charles himself puts it this way: 'I don't actually have a role to play. I have to create it, and there is no set of rules, so to speak, as to what my job is in the scheme of things. I am heir to the throne. Full stop. That is all. I could do absolutely nothing if I wanted to. I could go and play polo all over the world.

'All the interests I have got myself involved in I do because I am interested or concerned or anxious. I happen to mind about this country and I mind about all the countries of the Commonwealth. I can't affect things on a large scale. The only way I can see myself achieving anything is by example. One of the things that keeps me going all the time, I suppose, is that I can never, I believe, afford to sit back and I never could.'

The danger is that a Prince who is 'interested, concerned, anxious', who minds 'about this country and the countries of the Commonwealth', who feels that he cannot 'afford to sit back' and, indeed, has no desire to do so, may sooner or later become frustrated if his role is confined merely to setting an example— the more so if setting an example fails to achieve things. Charles himself has expressed disappointment that hitherto he has been mainly renowned for his polo-playing, shooting, steeplechasing and being kissed by admiring young ladies. It is an image he would very much like to discard. But the problem which faces him is that which has confronted successive heirs to the throne ever since princes were no longer called upon to ride into battle

at the head of armies. It is the question of how to establish a
wider and more worthwhile role while waiting in the wings of
monarchy.

Unlike Queen Victoria, Queen Elizabeth II would not object
if her eldest son could find and establish an individual role for
himself. It is the form that role should take which creates the
problem. Charles' own view that his role is what he chooses to
make of it is perhaps not completely valid. It may be true that
there is no set of written rules he is required to follow, but there
are unwritten rules, mostly negative, which can cut across what
he might like to do. He might have carved out a worthwhile
career in the Royal Navy had there not been objections to his
flying. It was the flying side of naval life which especially
appealed to him, but flying was considered too dangerous an
occupation for the heir to the throne. He would very much have
liked to have become Governor General of Australia, a country
for which he has long had special affection, but the return there
of a Labour government with republican aspirations effectively
ended that particular princely dream. In any event, as Sir John
Kerr's earlier action in dissolving the Australian Parliament
had shown, such appointments today have political overtones
which make them unsuitable for royal princes.

There have been discussions, more recently, with Prime
Minister Margaret Thatcher concerning the possibility of
finding a more positive role for the Prince of Wales. Such
discussions may yet bear fruit—may even have. done so by the
time this book is published. If they do not, then Charles will have
to content himself with achieving things 'by example', encouraging trade and industry, charity and the arts by his
continued patronage and occasional presence.

He may perhaps find his true niche as a patron of the arts. Not
since the days of the third and fourth Georges has there been a
member of the Royal Family with so passionate an interest in
the arts. Those Georges were great collectors: but for them, the
Royal Academy, the botanical gardens at Kew and even the
London Zoo would not now exist. Wealthy though he is by
ordinary standards, Charles could not afford to collect and
commission on the scale they did. Indeed, neither could George
IV always afford what he collected so enthusiastically, and he
was constantly in debt. In any event, Charles' taste lies more in
the direction of music. The Princess of Wales shares her

husband's enthusiasm. Their very first outing together after the announcement of their engagement was to the Royal Opera House. Their wedding was a positive festival of music. There have been frequent outings since to the opera, ballet, concerts and exhibitions of all kinds. They were together at an exhibition of Renaissance art the evening before it was announced that the Princess was pregnant with Prince William. Their fields of patronage embrace many facets of the nation's cultural and artistic life and doubtless will yet embrace many more.

At the time of his marriage to Diana Spencer, Charles had had nearly five years since leaving the Navy in which to adjust to and perfect his public role as Prince of Wales. It was a role towards which he had been trained, if only by example, almost from birth. The Princess came fresh and untrained to her distaff role, and if there was concern among her newly acquired royal in-laws as to how she would face up to it, it is scarcely to be wondered at. They need not have worried. The uncertain, puppy-fat teenager who, a week before her marriage, fled a polo ground in tears under the strain of finding herself the subject of so much public interest and photographic scrutiny, has changed almost out of recognition in the short time she has been Princess of Wales. So poised and polished has she become that she might have shared her husband's long years of training. Instead of tears, there are smiles and quips as she faces up to the crowds, the cameras and all the other daunting facets of the royal round. With only a few small hiccups and hang-ups along the way, already she has established herself as the new superstar of the royal roadshow. It has not all been as easy for her as she has made it appear. Her first year as a professional princess, coupled as it was to pregnancy, subject as she was—and still is—to a pressure of public popularity greater than any other member of the Royal Family has known, was especially difficult for her. That the pressure should have proved briefly too much for her, causing her to retreat to Highgrove, and within herself, is surely understandable. 'No one told me it would be like this,' she said of pregnancy. She might well have said the same of that first year of public life.

It is a very different Princess who has starred on the royal stage since the birth of Prince William. She is not only physically different, with a less chubby face and a new hair-do, but psychologically different, a young woman of strong character who has dug deep into her reserves to overcome the challenge of her royal role. 'I have learned a lot in the past few months,' she said midway through 1983. 'Particularly in the last three or four.' It is perhaps no more than an intriguing coincidence that part of those three or four months were spent in Australia, where her husband, Prince Charles, also recalls having undergone a curious metamorphosis when he was a raw prince, inexperienced in public life. He was seventeen at the time, shy and uncertain of himself in his royal role: crowds bothered him—and there was a crowd waiting to see him when his aircraft touched down at Brisbane. His own inclination was to remain out of sight in the aircraft while it refuelled, but those with him thought he should get out and show himself. 'I had to be virtually kicked out,' he remembers. Then, as he braced himself to quit the aircraft and walk towards the cheering crowd, it was as though 'something clicked inside me, and from that moment I have never felt nervous in public'. Perhaps one day, when his wife overcomes her distrust of the Press sufficiently to give interviews, it will be revealed whether she too experienced such a moment, and whether it was in Australia.

It was a fear of 'never again being free to act, speak or think as I really feel I should act, speak and think' which caused the Queen Mother, when she was an earl's daughter like Diana, twice to refuse, before finally accepting, the hand of a king's son. Sixty years on, Diana is in a far more vulnerable position. The newspapers of today are more intrusive than they were in the 1920s. Then there are the television cameras, zooming in close-up to reveal the slightest trace of uncertainty, embarrassment or boredom. The crowds on public occasions are bigger, more frenetic and more demanding. Her most private moments have already been the subject of public gossip and newspaper speculation, and will continue to be so. Her private life is the subject of endless rumour, frequent half-truths and occasional distortion. Are there strains in the marriage? Is she suffering from anorexia nervosa? Is she expecting another baby? Popular, worshipped almost, as she is, there is bound to be criticism at times.

A rifle shot in the hills above Balmoral brought the first ripple of criticism when her marriage to Charles was barely more than two months old. Turning over a gift salver in Wales to see if it was hallmarked resulted in more ripples. A commendable, if stumbling, attempt to speak Welsh was castigated as 'a sop'. In Australia and Canada, though the crowds went wild, fashion critics sniped at her clothes. Inevitably, there will be more criticism of like kind in the future, more rumour, more gossip, and some of it, to a person as sensitive as Diana, will hurt.

But for every critic and rumour-monger, there will be a horde of loyal admirers quick to spring to her defence. A shopkeeper so lacking in taste as to display a spoof nude of her in his window—it was her face but someone else's body—ended up with bricks shattering his glass. While hardly to be commended, the action is understandable in light of the niche the Princess has carved for herself in the hearts of so many people.

It is interesting to speculate upon the possible course of her life if Charles had not fallen in love with her or if she had shied away from his proposal of marriage. Attractive and affectionate as she is, she would presumably have married some other young man with no more pomp and ceremony than attended the weddings of her two sisters, the actual wedding day diminished from a worldwide television spectacular to a brief notice in the more up-market newspapers and a photograph or two in the glossier magazines. From then on, married life would have been an entirely personal affair, with none of the problems and plaudits of public life which go with her role as Princess of Wales. On this purely personal level it would probably have been very little different from the sort of life she still lives when away from the public spotlight. The essentials would be much the same, a country home, a nanny for baby, shopping in local stores, skiing holidays in winter. But because she did not marry an ordinary young man, because she married the Prince of Wales, that home in the country is stiff with security. When she pops out to the shops, an armed bodyguard must go with her. A trip to the ski slopes means running the gauntlet of myriad photographers. And while she may well bring up William herself while he is still a small child, later—because he is destined to be a future king—monarchy will assuredly take over.

William's upbringing is unlikely to differ much from that of his father. In childhood, because his mother is not Queen, he may see more of her, enjoy more of her attention, than Charles did of his. As he grows into boyhood, differing parental views will perhaps have to be resolved. Charles, from an early age, was raised in the riding-shooting-fishing tradition of royal males. He sat his first pony at the age of three, shot his first grouse at ten, his first stag soon after. Like most fathers, he will doubtless wish to raise his son as a real 'chip off the old block'. Diana, nervous of horses since she was thrown in childhood, not enthused by blood sports despite her country upbringing, may see things differently. But though doubtless she will experience that lump-in-the-throat feeling on the day she realizes that her firstborn is now a boy rather than a baby, she will not object when he goes off to boarding school. After all, she went to boarding school herself and enjoyed the experience perhaps more than her husband did. Boarding school for Prince Charles' generation was Prince Philip's idea. No previous monarch-in-the-making, not even the Queen, had ever been to school. Initially at least, Charles by no means enjoyed the experience, but, looking back, he is aware now of how much he benefited from it. The choice of schools for William will almost certainly be left to his parents. But later, because he is heir to the throne, other fingers will need to dabble in the educational pie.

Charles was still a schoolboy at Gordonstoun when a conference attended by the top brass of Government, Church and Armed Services was convened at Buckingham Palace to discuss his future. He himself was not present; nor were his views sought. The consensus of opinion was that he should go to university after Gordonstoun, then to the Royal Naval College at Dartmouth, then into the Royal Navy, all of which he did. There will doubtless be the same sort of conference when William, in turn, approaches his coming-of-age, and almost certainly much the same sort of outcome.

The boy's aptitude or inclinations are likely to have little relevance. However intelligent William may prove to be, however much of his parents' enthusiasm for music may have rubbed off on him, he will have no more chance of pursuing a scientific, academic or musical career than his father had of becoming the farmer he says he would have liked to have been. Science or music will necessarily be relegated to the sidelines of worthwhile hobbies. Training for future kingship must and will take precedence. Indeed, should William prove to be intellectually above average, he will do well to keep the fact hidden. The British are not fond of intellectual monarchs, as Queen Victoria's husband, Albert (who was king in everything but name), was to discover. A century and a half on, this is still true.

The qualities required of a future king are that he should be manly without being too macho, dutiful without being dull, courteous without being condescending, sensitive without being sentimental, and no more than averagely intelligent. He must also, the way monarchy has developed, have a ready line in banter, be able to shake hands by the hundred, not object to being kissed and have the ability to treat every tree-planting, ship-launching and statue-unveiling, however often repeated, as though he is doing it for the first time and thoroughly enjoying every moment. In brief, he must be all things to all people. No easy feat. But one thing is certain: with such loving, caring parents as Charles and Diana, William is assured of the best possible start to his preordained life.

Index